The

Coffee 'n' Cake

Club

The
Coffee 'n' Cake
Club

A sort-of memoir by

Lee Janogly (who?)

To my lovely sister
MARILYN
who is always there
to hold my hand

Contents

Intro.....

Me – a writer? Nah.

I never intended to write this book. I never intended to write my previous three books either. The words came into my head and suddenly appeared on my computer. Come to think of it, I never intended to be a writer at all.

It all started when I happened to be idling through a newspaper one day and noticed a competition. This was around the early 1960s when I was stuck at home with a baby and a toddler and bored out of my mind.

At that time, as well as the *Evening Standard*, there was another daily paper, the (long defunct) *Evening News*, and they were inviting readers to watch a television programme of their choice and send in a review of the programme. The one selected for printing each day would win ten shillings.

I thought 'why not'? There are only so many times you can sing 'The wheels on the bus go round and round' – not to mention spending a whole morning cooking a carrot and a sprig of broccoli and mashing them into an indescribable mess for some baby to spit in my hair.

There were only two television channels to choose from in those days so everyone watched more or less the same programmes. I wrote a review of a comedy show on my typewriter and posted it – the only means of communication in those days.

My review was published and I duly received a postal order (remember those, Reader?) for ten shillings. Good. Let's have another go. I sent in another review – and there it was in the paper. Another ten shillings. I'd earned a pound. This was a doddle.

After the third one was published, I received a phone call from the features editor of the *Evening News*. I remember his name – it was Nick Cole, as in Old King …

He said, 'Look' (I subsequently discovered he started every sentence with the word 'Look'). 'Look,' he said, 'your entries are by far the best but we can't keep giving the prize to the same person. It's not fair, so please desist.'

Ah! Nooo. I had grown rather attached to those postal orders, so I started sending in reviews using a variety of names, hoping no one would notice how many different people lived at the same address.

They did. I received another phone call from Mr Cole. 'Look,' he said, 'there's no point calling yourself Arabella Waterbucket, we know it's you, so get lost.' (Not in so many words but that was the drift.)

I had no choice. But a few weeks later, there was a strike of technicians at the BBC television centre and all you saw when you turned on was a blank screen with the words *'Due to industrial action, there will be no programmes broadcast at this time.'*

So I wrote a review of it. I put how much I loved the tranquillity of the programme, the beautiful music, how the black letters of the notice stood out so clearly against the brilliant white background and how upset I was to be going out that evening and would miss the next episode.

They loved it. Apparently, they passed it round to all the departments and I was summoned to the phone once again by Mr Cole. 'Look', he said, 'you're very original and we'd like you to submit a review twice a week, any programme you like, and we'll pay you 12s 6d for each one. How's that?' Fine by me.

He ended that call by saying five words that stuck with me: 'You should write, you know.' So I did …

1

'Did you know Winston Churchill, Grandma?'

You know you're old when you look at a 50p coin and think, 'That used to be ten shillings in old money'. Maybe your conversation is peppered with remarks like, 'What's that actor's name again?' and 'Why is he mumbling?'. But when do you actually realise that you are, shall we say, way beyond the first flush of menopause and probably in the final quarter of your life?

For me, this was when I was presented with a cake with the numbers '8' and '0' on it and I thought, 'Goodness, that is a big number, I must now be officially old'. Or was it when that nice young man offered me a seat on the tube and I thought, 'Hang on, I can hold the plank for five minutes, I'm probably fitter than you are, mate!'. But I just smiled and thanked him and sat down. (For the uninitiated, the 'plank' is an exercise pose that requires strong abdominal muscles.)

Like most people my age, I don't *feel* old, but then I don't know what 'old' is meant to feel like. Age is just something that happens year by year and you are usually only reminded of it by the reactions of others: the horror of a 'surprise' 50th birthday party or people who assume everyone with grey hair is either deaf or stupid and must be spoken to accordingly.

However, nothing beats the forceful reminder of your approaching decrepitude than grandchildren. I have been asked on occasion:

'Were you excavated during the war, Grandma?'

'What's a cassette?'

'Who's Frank Sinatra?'

A small visitor was fascinated by my landline. 'But that means you have to stand in one place to talk to someone,' she mused, puzzled.

I decided to ask some of my similar-aged friends when they discovered they were old. We are a group of seven or eight women and meet every Wednesday morning for 'coffee 'n' cake', taking turns to host. We've been friends for as long as any of us can remember and although, sadly, we have lost one or two members to cancer over the years, including some husbands, others have joined and we have formed firm and supportive friendships.

We do like a good gossip and adhere to the old adage, 'If you can't say anything nice then come and sit by me!'

This week the meeting was at my house – lemon drizzle since you ask. Between you and me, I may have added a bit too much 'drizzle' so it's more of a lemon pudding, but never mind. Anyway, I felt entitled to ask the question: when did you realise you were old?

My friend Deely said she definitely felt old when she fell over in the tube. Her real name is Delia but she is never called that because, as she admits, 'people assume I can cook'.

'I tripped over the wheels of one of those great trunks they cart around,' she said. 'People rushed to pick me up and settle me in a seat. I felt so embarrassed.'

This doesn't surprise any of us as Deely has a habit of falling over; you can be walking along with her, chatting amiably, then suddenly realise you are talking to empty air and look behind to see her prone on the pavement. She has fallen over at a wedding, on a cruise ship, in Zara and, conveniently, at the local hospital. Miraculously, she never seems to hurt herself or break anything, probably due to years of practice and a generous supply of adipose tissue (you can't say 'fat' any more) to cushion the fall – but being her friend is slightly unnerving.

My oldest friend, Nancy, piped up how she was in a café with her sister and gestured towards a couple of much older-looking women sitting at a table nearby. 'That's us in ten years' time,' she opined, and was horrified when her sister pointed out that it was a mirror. 'I didn't have my glasses on,' Nancy protested.

Laila and her husband moved to my neighbourhood from Iran in 1976. As a student, Laila was a friend of Farah Diba, who went on to become the second wife of the much older Shah Mohammed Reza Pahlavi. They met when they were both studying architecture in Paris and Laila was a guest at their wedding in Tehran where she met her future husband. The girls lost touch with each other when Laila came to England and, three years later, Farah and her husband were exiled to Egypt when Ayatollah Khomeini took over the country.

Laila said she was walking with her daughter and grandson when her daughter asked why she was limping. 'I didn't realise I was,' said Laila, 'until I looked down and saw I was wearing odd shoes, each with a different heel height! I thought "that is such an old lady thing to do" – but at least they were the same colour – almost. My embarrassment was compounded by my grandson saying, "I bet you've got another pair just like that at home, Grandma." Grrr!'

Sheila-Round-the-Bend (RTB) was cross with her doctor. She is known as Sheila-Round-the-Bend not because she's loopy (although … ?) but because her house is round the corner from mine. This is to distinguish her from another local friend of the same name who is known as Sheila-Down-the-Road (DTR) for obvious reasons. Sheila RTB is a psychotherapist, who had a bit of therapy herself at some point in her life and thought 'this is easy-peasy, I could do this' and promptly – or not so promptly – qualified as a therapist, though whether she adheres to the rigorous standards imposed by the British Association for Counselling and Psychotherapy (BACP) is not for me to say.

Anyway Sheila, who is 74, went to her doctor with a bothersome symptom. She was accompanied by her daughter as they were going shopping afterwards. Once seated, the doctor put on his kind, sympathetic face and enquired of *her daughter*, 'So how has she been lately?' Sheila raised her hand and said, 'Helloo doctor, I'm here. I'm not deaf or senile and can speak for myself.' He had the grace to look slightly abashed.

The other Sheila (DTR) interjected by saying, 'I always feel better when the doctor tells me my symptoms are normal for my age, but then I think dying will be normal for my age at some point.' Quite.

My very attractive friend Pauline was a classically trained actress before she married, and appeared in many films, usually as the sultry mistress of a married man, meaning she had to snog a lot of well-known actors – most of whom are now dead (not her fault!). Once her children were grown and had lives of their own, she thought she looked pretty good for her age and ventured back timidly into the profession, joining an agency that cast actors for TV adverts. After her eighth audition for incontinence pads, a chair-lift company or the 'before' face of a wrinkle cream, she gave up.

Recalling old films, I advised them not to revisit old films or programmes they loved when young. As a vulnerable 17-year-old in 1956, I saw a film (not a 'movie') called *The Eddy Duchin Story*, starring Kim Novak and the very handsome Tyrone Power, who played the title role of the famous pianist and band leader. The music featured throughout the film was Chopin's beautiful *Nocturne in E-Flat*, but not the way Fred C wrote it, as on this occasion it merited the full orchestral 20-musician arrangement with sweeping strings soaring to the ceiling. I fell in love with the music, the actors, the story, and wept buckets at the end of it.

The title jumped out at me when I noticed it was showing on one of the TV channels that specialised in old films and I sat down to watch it eagerly. And do you know what? It's the biggest load of schmaltzy rubbish you could imagine! Kim Novak was so wooden she practically had splinters, and the dialogue was trite. But the music was still wonderful and the film worth watching just for that.

We agreed that at least there was no graphic violence or close-up sex scenes in those days, which are difficult to avoid today. We've all had our fill of horrific torture scenes and the sight of heaving naked buttocks.

Barbara, a doctor's wife, had a more optimistic view by saying that fortunately attitudes were changing towards many things and jokes about race, skin colour and sexual orientation are frowned upon.

'With the exception being old age!' said Laila. 'These so-called comedians have no compunction in making jokes about frailty, incontinence, deafness or cognitive impairment, and couldn't care less for the feelings of anyone afflicted by these things.'

Another member of the group, Jess, chimed in. 'You're right! A couple of years ago I was watching that satirical programme *Have I Got News for You* which featured a well-known, long-haired comedian as guest panellist. For some reason he decided to give his impression of an old person eating an ice cream. He hunched over, screwed up his face and mimicked licking an imaginary cornet, making disgusting slurping noises. Why? To get a cheap laugh? No one I know eats ice cream like that. His mother must be very proud.'

'Well that just goes to show the dearth of his material,' said Laila.

We decided other things that should be banned from being shown on TV were people vomiting, especially when we were watching with a tray of food on our laps, characters cleaning their teeth (who walks around chatting while they're cleaning their teeth?) and any contestant in a music competition singing *Somewhere Over the Rainbow*.

Listening to them chat, I thought to myself that maybe some of us are a bit scatty, but all these women and other older people of my acquaintance, mostly in their 70s and 80s, are far from the slow, dim-witted geriatrics they are often portrayed to be. Their days are filled with looking after grandchildren in the school holidays, going to the gym, doing charity work or taking courses in everything from art appreciation to psychology. We are not all sitting at home knitting covers for our hot water bottles.

Many of us are much-loved grandparents who are enjoying watching the present generation growing up while confessing how glad we are that we are not raising children in this climate of mobile phones, 'wokeness' and the internet. All we can hope for, as they grow and become more discerning, is that our young charges will learn that life is a continuum from young to old and, regardless of age, all we want is for everyone to adhere to the Aretha Franklin song and be treated with 'Respect – just a little bit'.

What do you think, Reader? Come and join our chat. Coffee?

2

With friends like these …
you're lucky

'Why is it always me?' demanded Barbara about her friend Celia. 'We've known each other for 30 years but it's always *me* who has to contact *her* to make arrangements to meet. She's fine when we do get together but I'm fed up with always being the one to get in touch.'

We agreed that was annoying. The Wednesday meeting was at Deely's flat and she had made Nigella's recipe for clementine cake. 'It's got no flour in it!' she said proudly, which was fairly obvious as it was a bit squidgy – in fact it tasted like boiled clementines, which it basically was! Barbara went on grumbling, 'You know what? I decided a few weeks ago that I was going to wait for her to call me and I'm still waiting! I really can't be bothered.'

That got me thinking about friendships and those that are worth hanging onto and others that just naturally fade and wither. The 'keepers' are often like Nancy and me, who have been friends since we sat together watching our 3-year-old daughters trying vainly to comply with the ballet teacher's instructions to 'point your toes nicely'. Trying not to laugh as we watched these two little pumpkins trundle round the room, we had no illusions about whether they would end up in the *corps de ballet*!

Our friendship has endured ever since, and the girls, now in their 50s, are still friendly, as are *their* children, though none pursued a career in dance. Sheila DTR moved into her house the same year as I did, 1962 – then she was just known as Sheila – and Pauline joined our Wednesday group when her husband left her after having an affair with the lady who was teaching them to play bridge. He gave her a diamond and she gave him her heart and Pauline wanted to 'club' him with a spade. (Sorry Reader, couldn't resist.) Soon our little group expanded due to a love of baking – and consuming – cakes. We are proof that the bond between women can coalesce into a lasting support system which endures for years as they share all the joys and sorrows that life throws at them.

Of course we all have our own foibles and idiosyncrasies, none more so than our friend Jessica, whom I've known since we were both engaged to our future husbands. Although Jess is the kindest, most generous person you could possibly meet, since her husband died nine years ago she has become – how shall I put this? – one of those women who are never happier than when they are complaining about something. It could be anything from roadworks to the weather; in fact, if she had a Twitter account, which she doesn't, she would be in her element and could join all the others who are perpetually offended.

Her complaining manifests itself most obviously in restaurants, as wherever she is sitting is either too near the air-conditioning, the toilet or the kitchen, and there is bound to be something wrong with the food. For this reason we, as her friends, always insist that *she* chooses the restaurant herself, if occasion arises, so she can take responsibility for the ambience.

Recently I made the mistake of volunteering to take Jess out for lunch at a venue close to my home. I felt sorry for her as she was taking a long time to recover from a hip replacement operation and was still walking with a stick two months later. I asked another close friend, Gloria, to come with me for support and we arrived early, choosing a nice table by the window. Jess turned up clutching not only her stick but a padded backrest as she had a touch of sciatica as well.

She proclaimed the table we had chosen was too draughty so we traversed the room several times, with Jess trying to avoid hitting the other diners with her bag, coat, stick and backrest and not always succeeding. Gloria and I trailed behind until she found a satisfactory location.

Once we were all settled and Jess had found a suitable object to put under one of the table legs to stop it wobbling, she turned her attention to the cutlery and glasses for marks or stains, ready to demand substitutions if necessary. Fortunately there were none, which was lucky because, even when not complaining, Jess has a slight petulant tone in her voice that makes even a compliment sound like an accusation.

There was 'nothing she fancied' on the menu, but finally chose a dish with her own amendments: could she have creamed spinach instead of the chips and leave out the roasted tomatoes, and no beetroot on the salad – leaving the poor waiter totally confused. Oh, and could he take away the butter and bring some virgin olive oil instead to dip the bread into. Thank you. Oh, and sparkling water but no ice. Or lemon.

That settled, we started to chat and catch up with all the latest gossip, which in the case of Jess and Gloria meant indulging in a game of what I privately call 'competitive ailments'. Each one has, or knows someone who has, some terrible medical condition and try and outdo each other with tales of pain and suffering. They know the 'top man' in Harley Street for every part of the body – which actually can be very helpful at times, especially the ones to avoid, like that spinal surgeon who left that poor woman paralysed after a simple procedure.

This lasted until the starters arrived and Jess complained to the waiter that the music was so loud we couldn't hear ourselves speak and could he please turn it down. We then admired pictures of all 400 of Gloria's grandchildren on her phone.

Jess liked to finish her meal with a cup of green tea – weak, decaffeinated, preferably organic – which on this occasion was sent back because the cup was chipped. The waiter brought a fresh cup but unfortunately as he approached the table he banged into Jess's stick and a few drops of the tea slopped into the saucer. He took one look at Jess's face and veered in a swift 180-degree turn back to the kitchen.

Whereas in most restaurants it's impossible to catch the waiter's eye when you want to pay the bill, on this occasion he was hovering, machine in hand, just willing us to leave before Jess made any further demands.

Why do I put up with this? Well, as I mentioned earlier, Jess and I have known each other since we met at a mutual friend's house all those years ago and have shared the joyous births of children and grandchildren and the pain and grief of each losing our husbands. I realise I have painted her as a total nightmare, but she can be good company with a nice ironic sense of humour on occasion. It would be strange not to have her in my life. When the whingeing gets too much we all just shrug and say to each other 'you know what she's like'.

On this occasion we parted with hugs and promises to do this again very soon. Maybe I'll adopt the late comedian Peter Cook's excuse when he didn't want to go somewhere. 'I'm planning to watch television that night'.

Barbara is still waiting for her friend Celia to call.

3

Growing up with a Jewish mother

I was early for our Wednesday meeting at Barbara's house and found her in the kitchen washing up the breakfast things. A freshly baked cake looked enticingly at me from the table.

'It's a yoghurt cake', she said, 'the easiest cake ever. You just throw all the ingredients into one bowl, using the yoghurt pot as a measure once you've tipped out the contents. One pot of vegetable oil, two sugar, three flour, three eggs. Bingo! Done.'

I was sure there was more to it than that and offered to help her get the coffee things together.

'You could put the milk in a jug,' said Barbara, but as I picked up the carton it leaked all over the worktop. She fetched a cloth to mop it up and I reached for a tea towel to help her dry the dishes.

'Not that one!' she shrieked. 'That's for the dog's bowl. Look, why don't you just sit quietly over there and wait for the others.'

I did as I was told, and her remark instantly propelled my memory back to the old-fashioned kitchen of my childhood:

'You're using the wrong tea towel!' my mother shouted at me. This was 1947 and, as a mere 8-year-old, I was attempting to be helpful by drying the newly washed cups on the draining board. 'The red one is for *meat*, you should be using the blue one for *milk*.'

In trouble again. I was the bad one who could do nothing right. My sister, four years my junior, was the perfect child – as she keeps smugly reminding me to this day.

Not mixing meat and milk – which extends to tea towels – is just one of the many quirks of the Jewish religion, and my mother kept them all – religiously (ha!). If a 'meat' knife accidently came into contact with some butter ('milk', geddit?) it had to be buried in the garden for 24 hours to 'purify' it, much to the puzzlement of the gardener. I told him we were growing a cutlery tree.

If she didn't stick to these rituals, my mother was convinced God would punish her. She lived by two maxims: 'What will people think?' and 'Doing the right thing'. She was highly critical of others whom she perceived of as not 'doing the right thing'. What was this 'right thing'? Whatever she decided it was.

In those days it was normal for the wife to stay at home raising the children and the husband to be the breadwinner. My father was in what was known as the 'fur trade' – not the retail side but as a 'fur dresser' in a factory in the East End of London, a business set up by his father in the 1930s. Bunches of dead mink were delivered to the factory and their fur was harvested and turned into the gleaming pelts ready to be made into fashionable fur coats. Ugh! The very thought of it makes me feel nauseous and I've never been able to wear anything trimmed with real fur. But in those days, wearing a fur coat was a sign of affluence and greatly desired. Old films show a moustachioed gangster draping a fur stole round the shoulders of his young mistress, with her exhibiting the sort of ecstasy equivalent to receiving a Chanel or Hermès handbag today.

I guess the fur trade was quite a lucrative business to be in in those days, affording our family a fairly decent standard of living including a holiday in the South of France every year. Eventually, thanks to organisations petitioning against animal cruelty, the wearing of fur dwindled and the business was sold, accompanied by a similar dwindling of the family finances, and my father became a minicab driver.

However, nothing would stop my mother adhering to her values. Take white gloves: when you go to the synagogue, which we did every Saturday, you had to wear a pair of clean, white gloves which had to remain spotless. I don't know if this is written in the Torah, but it's 'doing the right thing'. Being a rebel, I would trail my hands along the railings as we walked to the synagogue so they were filthy by the time we got there. I'm still waiting for God to punish me for that.

I say 'as we walked to the synagogue' but we lived in Finchley, North London, and my grandparents, to whom we went for lunch every week after the service, lived in Brondesbury Park, which was a fairly affluent area in the forties but several miles from our house. This caused a huge dilemma for my mother as you were not supposed to drive, or indeed use any form of transport, on the Sabbath, so how would we get there? My father would leave early and drive to his parents' house and leave the car there and walk with them to the local synagogue – but in their eyes that wasn't cheating.

My mother could never get herself, and me and my sister, ready in time to go with him – what with faffing around with white gloves etc. – so we went by taxi, hoping God wouldn't notice, or reasoning that she had been punished enough by having a daughter like me. My mother made the taxi driver stop round the corner from the synagogue and we walked the few remaining yards. Obviously, the rabbi and entire congregation would be horrified if they knew we had driven there. What would people think?

My mother had never learned to drive so we shared a driver with my grandparents who were too old to drive. He was called by his surname, Avis, even by us children – the thought of which makes me cringe today. (Mr) Avis came each day to take us to school then take my mother to Selfridges – presumably to buy more white gloves. On the way to school, we would pick up a few of my classmates who coerced Avis into placing bets on horses for them, which he obligingly did. Eventually my mother learned to drive, so it was goodbye Avis – to the detriment of the local betting shops.

On Fridays, my mother didn't go to Selfridges. She would spend the whole day preparing for the Sabbath which started at nightfall and continued the following day. This meant making copious amounts of the traditional Sabbath fare of chopped liver, chicken soup and roast chicken. So that she didn't have to cook on Saturdays (not allowed) she would fry enough fish to feed the entire neighbourhood, ready to be eaten cold with various salads over the weekend. She would do this swathed in a burka-style garment to protect her hair and clothes from the smell of frying, a courtesy she failed to extend to the rest of the house and its inhabitants.

The preparing-for-Sabbath Fry-day would always start with a crisis with my mother screaming on the phone to Mr Stoller, the fishmonger, as to the whereabouts of her delivery order.

This ritual continued all through my childhood and teenage years, and somehow I grew into a fully functioning adult, having survived this weekly hysteria reasonably intact. Once in possession of a home of my own, I amassed tea towels in a variety of hues which I used with total abandon. I rarely go to the synagogue as I don't own a pair of white gloves. If I want some chopped liver, I buy it ready-made at the kosher butchers. I guess I have my own version of 'doing the right thing' but I certainly wouldn't expect or impose it on others – and I couldn't care less what other people think.

However, I think it's important to support local family-run businesses, and old traditions die hard, so I still get my fish from Stoller's as it's the freshest in London (sometimes mothers DO know best!) – albeit from the granddaughter of the recipient of my mother's wrath. But I don't fry it.

4

Grumpy day/cheerful day

(Reader: Please excuse this tongue-in-cheek
chapter – I just felt like it, OK?)

Grumpy Day:

The Wednesday meeting was cancelled this week. It was meant to be at Jess's house but she called to say she didn't feel well, and after listening to her whingeing for half an hour about everything from her cleaner going back to Romania (is it beyond her to use a duster?) to her wayward son who 'never picks up the phone' (who can blame him?) it left me in a thoroughly bad mood.

I've decided if Jess can do it, so can I. I'm going to have a rant about things that bug me. I'm allowed to do this because being in my 80s makes me officially old – but don't dare call me an 'oldie'. What's an 'oldie'? I hate that word. I am also obviously a woman and as these two components are often preceded by the word 'grumpy', that is what I have decided to become: a grumpy old woman – at least for today.

My grumpiness often erupts in the supermarket, especially if the woman in front of me at the checkout has unpacked half her purchases on to the conveyor belt then realises she has forgotten something and disappears for what seems like *hours* while I stand there fuming and the poor cashier gives me a 'what-can-I-do' shrug.

She will eventually return clutching something like a sweet potato which is obviously a vital ingredient for some exotic dish she is cooking tonight. This is often followed by her mobile phone ringing which she obviously *has* to answer before completing her shopping transaction, making me feel like one of those cartoon characters who are pictured with steam coming out of their ears with frustration. Should she then compound this misdemeanour by asking her caller, 'Yes I've got the sweet potato, is there anything else you need while I'm here?' I'm gripped by a white-hot fury ready to erupt into 'Oh no lady, if you disappear again I will ram that trolley right up your ample arse!'

OK, calm down. Another irritation at the checkout is if I have done a substantial shop and whilst unloading my purchases from the trolley on to the conveyer belt, the person behind me starts placing theirs before I've finished, thereby taking up space that I need.

For these occasions I have perfected a glare which should reduce someone to a withered husk as they sink to the floor in shame but seems to leave that sort of person totally oblivious. My only course of action is to grab the little portable barrier separating our shopping and ram it against her Persil so hard it falls back into her trolley. Oh, sorry.

Loud music in the hairdressers. Why?

'Would you mind turning the music down, please?'

'Sorree, what did you say?'

Precisely.

Then the chat:

'You doin' anyfink nice this weekend?'

'Yes, I'm going to have tea with Meghan and Harry and take photos of their children to sell to the newspapers.'

'Reelly?'

No.

I know I should keep up with the modern variations of language but can't help experiencing a nudge of irritation when out for a meal with my older grandchildren and their friends and they use the phrase 'Can I get' when ordering, as in 'Can I get a pepperoni pizza and a coke'. What happened to 'May I have' and even 'Please'?

OK, I know I'm not the most grammatical of writers but why, when I email my thanks to a youngish person for some service, do I get the reply 'Your welcome' – spelt y-o-u-r. This seems to be considered universally correct by even the highest honours graduate. And don't get me started on 'sat', as in 'I was sat under a tree' or whatever. For some reason that drives me nuts. What's wrong with 'sitting' or even 'seated'?

Mobile phones – another bugbear! Idiots glued to this object held to their faces as they stroll across the road in front of my car inevitably as the light turns green. I actually enjoy seeing them nearly jump out of their skin as I blast my horn. As for that young woman who pushed her buggy *with her small child in it* into the road between two parked cars with her free hand looking at her phone, it's a good thing I managed to stop in time. And she glared at *me* – like it was my fault I nearly killed her kid!

Computers: 'Please insert your password'. I have. 'Your password has not been recognised, please try again'. I did. 'Please call the helpline'. I tried. 'We are experiencing a high volume of calls at the moment, please try again later'. No. Get lost!

Why do people insist on using acronyms in texts and emails all the time? I have no idea what most of them stand for. Like David Cameron texting to his friend Rebecca Wade, I thought LOL meant 'lots of love'. Wrong! WTF! It's a wonder anyone gets anything accomplished today they are so busy on Twitter, Facebook, Instagram, TikTok, YouTube and all the rest of the time wasters.

Inept politicians, roadworks blocking every road to my destination, cancel culture (how dare they!) You know what? I think I need a nice lie down …

Cheerful Day:

The sun is shining and I've decided I'm going to have a lovely, happy day. This should be easy as every year that goes by, I find myself becoming more patient and tolerant of the world around me. My motto is: 'Don't be sad that roses have thorns, be happy that thorns have roses.' Isn't that sweet?

I like to look for the good in people. For instance, I'm sure that young man who drove forwards into the parking space I was about to back into had a much more import-ant appointment to get to than I did. I hope he has a good day. I smiled at him and he gave me a cheery wave with his middle finger.

I love going to the supermarket. Such an array of wonderful things to buy. I was standing behind a young mum at the checkout and admired the fourteen bottles of sparkling cola drink in her trolley – so full of vitamins. She must have very happy children. I really didn't mind that she was on her phone, I was quite happy to wait, although the checkout lady didn't look too pleased as she was waiting for her to pay. I smiled at her to try and convey that I understood this is what young people do today and she was probably having a lovely chat with a friend, or even her mother.

I don't normally listen to people's telephone conversations but she was speaking quite loudly and apparently the poor girl is having trouble sleeping because the words 'fucking nightmare' were repeated quite a lot. Oh dear. I was admiring the large tattoo on her neck. It was of a dragon with a dead rat hanging out of its mouth. Utterly charming. Maybe I should consider getting one myself. I mean you have to keep up with young people nowadays, don't you?

Oh, she's getting her credit card out to pay even though she hasn't finished her conversation yet. Isn't that thoughtful?

Another favourite place of mine is the hairdresser's where I go every Tuesday. They play such lovely music there, really up-to-date stuff and nice and loud, showing real consideration to their deaf clients. I asked the young girl washing my hair if she knew the name of the group singing one of the songs. She said she hadn't a clue and asked her colleague at the next basin. I didn't quite catch her answer but I think it was something like 'Silly old Bat' which is a strange name for a group, isn't it? They are such lovely girls.

I think I'll go and see my grandchildren on my way home. My daughter-in-law loves it when I pop in unexpectedly, especially when she is preparing their supper so I can help her. Do you know, she asks each child what they want to eat, then cooks a different meal for each one. Wonderful. I never did that. This generation of parents is so much more attuned to their children's needs.

While my daughter-in-law was busy at the stove, I told her how her husband – my special boy – was the perfect child and even at three years old would sit at the table holding his knife and fork properly. She knew I didn't mean it as a criticism, even though Joshi-Noshi was eating with his fingers at the time, because she gave me one of her sweet clenched-teeth smiles. (I might have told her that story before, I can't remember.) She is such a lovely girl, we get on much better now.

My teenage granddaughter was very appreciative when I told her she would look so much better with her hair tied back and not all over her face. She told me her favourite singer is someone called Megan Thee Stallion. Isn't that a pretty name? I asked if she sang any songs from *The Sound of Music* and she said probably. It's so important to keep up with young people nowadays so I asked her how many 'likes' she got on her Tittygram account and she did that cute little thing they do, shaking her head while raising her eyes to the ceiling. She's adorable.

They've all got their mobile phones and iPads on the table next to them in case they have to look up something important. Children today are so well-informed and know about all the different sex positions and types of deviance from the brilliant, easily accessible porn sites – things that I never knew about until I was married. There's so much diversity in children's education today. Thank goodness they've abandoned teaching all that boring stuff like grammar and punctuation – so unnecessary.

Maybe when the children are older they can go to university and join in all the protest marches and pull down all those nasty statues that are cluttering up our cities. It looks such fun.

I do hope I'm setting a good example to them and they grow up to be as kind and patient as I am.

5

Pete the builder

There was a strong smell of paint as we trooped into Sheila RTB's house on a sunny Wednesday morning.

'Sorry, I thought the decorators would be gone by now.' She made a face. 'We had a leak in the roof and the water came through the ceiling. Once the ceiling was repainted we noticed the walls looked dingy, then the cupboards needed doing – and so on.'

Sheila led us through to the garden, warning Deely there were dustsheets protecting the carpet and she should be careful not to – too late. We helped her up, somehow unscathed as usual. The coffee things were laid out on a table, complete with her speciality, a gungy honey cake. It was moist and delicious. Apparently, the secret is to make it in advance, wrap it in tinfoil and forget about it for three weeks so it develops the right soft consistency. Sheila gave me the recipe once but there were so many ingredients I could have bought one for half the price. 'It might have an added flavour of emulsion and turps,' she warned.

'Is your decorator any good?' I asked, and she shrugged.

'I wouldn't know. He's from some Eastern European country and he's got such a thick accent I can't understand what he's saying so I just nod and agree with everything and hope for the best.'

I felt a twinge of guilt thinking I should do something about my own house which I have lived in for over 60 years. Every so often I look round and notice black smudges creeping up the walls from the heat of the radiators and paint flaking off the doors, particularly the door jamb in the kitchen where I ram a bottle or jar into it to twist off a stubborn lid.

On these occasions it's time to call in Pete the builder. Pete is an amiable man of average height with a squat, muscular body and blue eyes. He wears shorts all year round in all weathers and he must have had hair at some point in his life though, since being driven mad by members of my family for over twenty years, I can't remember ever seeing any sign of it.

Pete is not only a builder, painter and decorator, but also a plumber, electrician and carpenter. He does all of these moderately well, although there are sometimes little quirks – such as when you turn on a tap with red markings and wait in vain for some expected hot water to gush out, then turn on the tap with blue markings and nearly scald your hand. But nothing he has put up has ever fallen down, so that's something. Pete likes to start early, around 7am with 'milk and two sugars, please love', and leave at 3pm to collect his daughter from school. His wife is a nurse on various shifts.

Pete would follow me obediently around the house as I explained what needed to be done then said he would bring 'a couple of the lads' and get the job done 'in no time'.

Pete's concept of 'no time' is fairly accurate as it could be anything from two weeks to nine months. The problem being that, as well as copious amount of tea, he also liked chocolate digestive biscuits. Unfortunately so do I, and the size of my thighs increased in proportion to the amount of time Pete would take to finish the job. I think having builders in your home should closely follow death and divorce in the stress charts. After twelve weeks, my hips could be used to measure the width of the goalposts for the football pitch in the nearby playing fields.

I have no interest or talent for interior design. My mother chose my furniture when, newly married, I moved into the house, and any decisions thereafter regarding curtains, carpets or lampshades have been taken by my sister. This may explain the slight tension that exists between Pete and me regarding his use of the phrase 'It's up to you'.

For example, he will say, 'Where do you want that socket?' I will reply, 'I don't know, where do you suggest?' – and he will say, 'It's up to you.' He will ask, 'What colour paint to you want in that room?' 'Um, do you think that beigey one would be nice?' 'It's up to you.' Well, I'll just finish this packet of chocolate chip cookies then I'll phone my sister.

Pete and his 'lads' – seasoned men in their fifties – have a way of speaking that I seem to find peculiarly contagious. I find myself saying 'I fought you was goin' to fix them door 'andles.' My mother, who sent me to elocution lessons as a child, would have quaked with horror.

Is it just Pete or do all builders assume you need a running commentary of everything they are doing if you deign to enter the area under construction? 'See that little crack

– that means the interweaving crossover flange-sprocket has come loose and I may have to fit a reinforced cranial double-ratchet intersplit.' Really? 'Yeah.' Weary shake of head. 'In which case I'm going to need a Morton's rotary speculator with a G40 thrust nozzle.' Right. Fine. Whatever. 'I'll just nip dahn the yard and get one—' Adding ominously over his shoulder '—Don't touch that exposed wire, love,' before disappearing for three weeks.

I remember the time Pete sat down for his usual 'milk with two sugars, please love' and announced he was going on a diet, patting his now noticeable paunch. 'I'm only taking one and a half sugars in my tea now,' he said proudly, and demonstrated his steely resolve by breaking a sugar cube in half and putting one half in his cup. Not sure what to do with the other half, he put it in his mouth. I didn't comment except to attempt to remove the plate of biscuits from his – and my – grasp, but that was taking his diet a step too far. 'Maybe just one,' he murmured as we finished the plate between us.

Pete is a cheerful presence to have around the house and considers himself to be almost a member of my family. The only time I've seen him cry was when my husband died a few years ago. But as soon as his huge blue van turns into my drive, the neighbours on either side of my house appear like magic. 'Oh Peter, when you've got a minute …'

I would give you his number, Reader, but you may have to wait a long time because he is greatly in demand. But once you get hold of him, he'll do the job in no time.

6

The fickle fads of fashion

'What on earth am I supposed to wear?' cried Pauline as we gathered round her table one Wednesday morning. 'My granddaughter is getting married and the wedding is in Florence. That's Italy,' she added as nobody said anything.

'Yes we know,' I said, 'but why Italy?'

'Because the fiancé is Italian and, although they met here, all his family live in Florence so they decided to hold the wedding there. It's going to go on for a whole weekend and I've no idea what sort of clothes to take. There's plenty of advice for the mother of the bride, but I'm the *grandmother*! They'll probably sit me with all the other old biddies next to the speakers so we can't hear each other talk – so that takes care of the language problem.'

We all sympathised but couldn't really offer any advice, not knowing what sort of wedding it was going to be. We shifted our attention to Pauline's ginger cake with lemon icing instead. She had either added too much ginger or lemon because we all had a discreet choking fit after the first mouthful – but as Pauline was obviously struggling with her fashion dilemma no one said anything.

Looking around, I noticed that we all had our own style of dressing, which in my case was no style at all. Fashion can be a minefield at any age, but doubly so once you reach actual old age. It's mutton versus frumpy. Wearing anything too short or girly makes you look like a cross between the Sugar Plum Fairy and Barbie's grandmother. As you have invariably lost height over the years, wearing floor-length dresses presents an image of one of Snow White's little helpers.

How to get it right? How often have we looked at someone and wondered if they got dressed in the dark? Is grey-haired granny getting 'down with the kids' turning up at the school gate wearing ripped jeans or has she had a collision with an e-scooter on the way?

Some magazines try to be helpful with strident headlines on their front covers proclaiming: 'Fashion advice for older women'. It only takes a glance before realising their idea of 'older women' are those ancient old hags who've managed to keep breathing for half a century. 50! I've got nighties older than that! Yes, apparently once you reach 50 your fashion sense drops as sharply as your oestrogen levels.

At whatever age, all fashion advice states the importance of proper underwear and suitable foundation garments, notably a properly fitting bra. Apparently, most women don't always realise their shape changes as they get older and they continue buying the same size and cup-size for years. Not me! I remember all too well my mother taking my 12-year-old burgeoning buds to a local shop specialising in 'ladies' undergarments' to be fitted for my very first bra.

The shop was run by an ancient (in my eyes) Polish lady whose name consisted of so many Ss and Zs that no one could pronounce it, so she was known as Madame Zizi. I continued to frequent Madame Zizi's establishment – known affectionately as 'Bras R Us' – all through my adolescence, marriage and subsequent pregnancies, and always left feeling firm and uplifted in mind and breast. I was devastated when Madame Zizi died, and we all thought the enterprise would go bust (ha ha). Fortunately, her daughter stepped in to save the shop from going tits-up (heh!) and later various nieces were welcomed into the bosom of the family business (OK, I'll stop now). Seventy-five years later it's still going strong, in spite of running out of family members, although the new owners have now graduated to swimsuits and shapewear like Spanx.

They also sold ladies hosiery, which in those days meant nylon stockings. In our late teens, we all wore stockings under our skirts that had to be held in place either by an elasticated tube known as a 'panty girdle' or 'roll-on' – the precursor of today's Spanx – which straddled the lower trunk with dangling suspenders fore and aft to clip on to the stockings, or the lighter suspender belt, a thin strip of elastic worn round the waist but with the same appendages to hold up the stockings.

The former was the accepted uniform for my mother's generation as the panty girdle held in your stomach. However, it also squashed the whole hip area and all the women of that generation had flat bottoms which looked fine under the straight skirts they wore. A glimpse of Kim Kardashian would be viewed with horror. Very few women wore trousers except a few Hollywood actresses like Kathryn Hepburn and Lauren Bacall who were considered very daring. 'Trouser suits' were introduced in the 70s and my legs haven't seen the light of day since.

Stockings were a nightmare for all of us as they tended to snag on any rough piece of furniture or fingernail, and a small hole would travel up the length of the leg – unless it was stopped in its tracks by the hasty application of a blob of nail varnish. Seriously.

A boy's chat-up line, 'Can I climb up your ladder?' would double the mortification of not only having a 'run' in your stockings but that it was obviously noticeable. The relief was widespread when tights, initially called pantyhose, were invented in 1959 by incorporating elastic into the material, as finally we could do away with the cumbersome suspender belts and pull on a single garment. Unfortunately, the first ones were all a uniform colour, 'American Tan', and everyone walked around with orange legs.

Not everyone was happy about this new invention though, mainly men, as the perception of stockings with the associated use of flimsy lace, suspenders and the exposure of thigh were considered to be more sexy and alluring than tights. I've never understood this as in my group of friends our inner thighs are not the most cherished part of our anatomy.

That Wednesday at Pauline's, when we talked about Spanx and those elasticated horrors that are supposed to smooth out your fat by pushing it either up or downwards out of sight under clothes, I glanced at Nancy whom I know had an unfortunate experience some years ago.

'You tell them,' she said as the others looked at me enquiringly. 'It still brings me out in a cold sweat whenever I think of that night.'

As I remember it, Nancy's husband had been promoted to a senior position at his work and, as the company had had a good year, they decided to hold their annual Christmas party at a swanky London hotel instead of their usual restaurant and all the executive wives were included. This meant 'black tie' and, although Nancy was happy with her choice of dress, the few extra pounds she had gained around her middle during the summer had decided to cling on for the rest of the year. She shopped around and bought a 'waist clincher' – a firm, elasticated garment which smoothed out her tummy and whittled down her waist beautifully when she tried it on in the shop.

Nancy felt confident entering the hotel with her husband who immediately gravitated towards his colleagues and left her to chat to the wives that she knew. She didn't realise how many times the circulating waiters had filled up her champagne glass but, feeling slightly tipsy, she suddenly caught sight of herself in a mirror and, to her horror, the top of the waist clincher had rolled down and was forming an unattractive bulge of material encircling her body just below her ribs, which her companions had either failed to notice or were too polite to say anything.

She hastened to the loo and, in a fit of frustration, rolled the wretched thing down and off. It was too bulky to fit into her smart little clutch bag and she tried to sneak to her table to deposit it underneath to be retrieved later. At that moment, she caught her husband's eye and he signalled that he was bringing his new boss over to introduce him to her. Oh God! She looked around desperately, wondering where she could hide the offending garment, and sidled towards a potted palm tree where she deposited it behind the slender trunk.

Later, Nancy saw the head waiter questioning his staff about something, with each one shaking their heads as he held out – you've guessed it! She pretended not to notice.

Of course, we laughed while Nancy cringed but Pauline said she could top that for embarrassment. I'll let her tell it:

'I'd just come out the shower when my daughter Susie called in a panic saying her car wouldn't start and could I come and take little 5-year-old Tasmin to school. I only live ten minutes away so I quickly pulled on the nearest clothes to hand, bra, pants, jumper, skirt, and rushed out the door. We got to the school and I took Tasmin's hand and was walking up the drive when a voice behind me said, "Excuse me, I think you've dropped something". I turned, and one of the dads, looking a bit pink-faced, handed me a lacy thong which looked very much like the one I keep to wear under my Pilates leggings. I muttered my thanks, feeling my face turn a shade of deep scarlet as the poor man scarpered. In my haste, grabbing my knickers out of the drawer, the thong must have somehow attached itself to the back of them and I didn't notice until they dropped out of my skirt. Oh, the embarrassment!'

I guess these things happen and 'fashion malfunctions' have become a badge of honour for celebrities to relate on television chat shows. It's not pleasant when it happens to you, though, especially when you don't realise there is anything wrong – like Sheila RTB, who was out with her family one day and was wearing a T-shirt with the innocuous word 'SATURDAY' written across it. The day being a bit chilly, she popped on a cardigan and wondered why people kept staring at her, until someone pointed out that her cardie was covering the first two letters of the word on one side and the last two letters on the other …

7

Auntie Gertie

Nancy appeared to be in surprisingly good humour when she finally arrived at Laila's house – considering she had just been to a funeral.

'It was just so funny,' she said, helping herself to a slice of chocolate roulade (Laila is a brilliant cook). 'I didn't know Ralph, the deceased, very well but he was a real character. He must have been in his nineties and had married four times, each time ditching the current wife for a younger version of the same woman. I only went to support my cousin, Anne, who was wife number two. He was very wealthy and continued paying alimony to each of them, so they all turned up to the funeral and stood there glaring at each other. He even tried to marry his carer, having forgotten he was not officially divorced from wife number four. I really had to stop myself laughing. He was a one-off.'

We began discussing the unusual characters we had come across in our lives, but none could match mine when I was young. I guess every child has one eccentric aunt who livened up their childhood. Mine was Auntie Gertie. She wasn't really my aunt, although there was some convoluted family connection on my father's side through marriage.

Everything about Auntie Gertie was large, loud and flamboyant, from her magenta hair and matching lipstick to her eye-catching clothes and huge chunky jewellery. She would sweep into our house, trailing several floaty scarves, and shout from the doorway, 'Hellooo all you lovely people,' and everyone would stop what they were saying and look round. She was followed by her rather weedy husband who was half her size, both in height and width, with the anxious look of a puppy wondering whether it would be all right to pee on the carpet.

I think his name was Norris but as Auntie Gertie called him Shnooky, so did everyone else. She would order him about mercilessly. 'Shnooky, pass me my bag', 'Shnooky, be a dear and pour me a little whisky' (one of many 'little' whiskies), 'Shnooky, did you bring my cigarettes?'

Ah, the cigarettes. She smoked endlessly and as a child of seven or eight I was fascinated by the fact that she could talk for ages with a cigarette in her mouth. I would watch as it went up and down as she spoke, never leaving her lips unless she removed it to bellow with laughter, which happened quite often. She would then absentmindedly stub out the cigarette end in the nearest receptacle, be it a saucer, flower pot or leftover trifle.

Auntie Gertie was part of a strange family. There was an apocryphal story about when her father died, her brother Morty gave the eulogy at the funeral and said, 'I am comforted by the thought that my father died so peacefully in his sleep'. He paused and then (allegedly) added, 'unlike the three passengers in the car he was driving'. I'm sure that's not true.

However, Auntie Gertie's main claim to fame was her *gefilte* fish. This is a Jewish recipe made from minced raw fish and flavoured with grated onion, salt and pepper, beaten egg and various other additives, then formed into large balls or patties and either boiled or fried. She was an excellent cook and people would come from far and wide to taste and marvel at her *gefilte* fish. There was talk that Auntie Gertie must have some secret ingredient that she wasn't divulging to make her *gefilte* fish so special as it was the talk of the community and much in demand at charity dinners.

I was with my mother when we discovered what this secret ingredient actually was. We had popped in to her enormous house to return her gloves, which she had left behind, and found her in the kitchen hugging a huge bowl of minced fish to her chest with one arm and stirring it energetically with a wooden spoon with the other. As usual, the ever-present cigarette was in her mouth and, as she chatted away to us, I watched, fascinated, as bit by bit the ash dropped from the cigarette into the bowl to be stirred vigorously into the mixture. She seemed to be quite unaware of this, unconsciously adding the unique flavour to the fish for which she was so admired.

Auntie Gertie had an air of authority that was rarely questioned, but even she couldn't think up a plausible enough excuse to prevent her darling son, 'Sweetie-Pie Paulie', from being conscripted, and during the war he was reluctantly – on both sides – accepted into the Royal Navy. His older brother, 'Naughty-boy Normie', escaped being called up into the armed forces by dint of having flat feet. Paulie placated his mother by assuring her that being stuck on a ship at sea was the safest option, one removed from any dangerous action. The fact that he might be blown out of the water at any time was not a consideration.

On one occasion, Auntie Gertie heard that the Admiral of the Fleet was to inspect his troops before sailing and she packed up a hamper of all Sweetie-Pie Paulie's favourite food, including the fried version of her celebrated *gefilte* fish. She instructed her chauffeur to drive to the docks and hand it to the Admiral to give to Paulie. Whether the poor man succeeded in his mission or chickened out and fed his family for a week is not recorded.

As well as being an imaginative cook, Auntie Gertie was an extremely astute businesswoman and the driving force behind the family business which was supplying bricks and roofing tiles to the building trade. As the country was busy rebuilding after the war, this was a very lucrative enterprise and earned a huge amount of money for the family. In fact, Auntie Gertie was so well-known in the financial district that the Managing Director of Barclays Bank was a frequent visitor at her dinner table, being a connoisseur of her famous *gefilte* fish.

She would turn up at Barclays' Head Office in the City of London in her chauffeur-driven Rolls to discuss the business and barge through the door of the bank in a flurry of mink, perfume and floaty scarves. She waggled her scarlet-tipped fingers at the receptionist, who surely would have preferred to announce her arrival more formally, and waltzed straight past her to the manager's office. Once effusively greeted and seated, she would spread her papers all over his desk while he poured her a little whisky and they chatted for an hour before getting down to the matter in hand.

It was after one of those occasions when her phone rang at 11 o'clock that night. She answered to hear her friendly bank manager saying, 'Gertie my dear, I do apologise for the late hour but when you swept all your papers into your bag, you didn't by any chance include a large bunch of keys for the vault, the alarm and the front door of the bank which were on my desk? It's just that they are missing and we can't lock up.'

She retrieved her cavernous bag and looked inside and, sure enough, discovered a large bunch of strange keys. Luckily, her chauffeur was still on duty and she was able to return them to their rightful owner with the minimum of fuss.

I sort of lost touch with her as I grew up, although she did buy me a present of a beautiful 48-piece dinner service when I got married, which I still use to this day.

8

The family doctor

As all the members of our group are of a similar advanced age, the talk often turns to health and recurring ailments. We were at Jess's house one Wednesday and she had made Danish cinnamon buns. No, I don't either. I didn't say anything because Jess can be a bit touchy sometimes. She still hadn't completely recovered from her recent illness and was grumbling about her medical treatment.

'You've really got to shop around for a decent MRI nowadays,' she said. I noticed yet another box of tablets had joined her vast collection of medications lining her window sill, each one prescribed to alleviate the side-effects caused by the previous one. This possibly started with some minor ailment and escalated into the current situation, but Jess really loves her array of pills, tablets and ointments and takes or applies them randomly whenever she feels like it.

Being old wives, the conversation turned to 'old wives tales' – those cures that you don't get from a doctor but have been handed down through generations of women.

Nancy insisted that her mother's recipe for chicken soup was the ultimate cure for colds and flu. 'There is now written evidence that it works,' she said. 'Scientists have proved that chicken soup reduces inflammation in the lungs.'

Deely wanted to know how the scientists knew Nancy's mother.

Sheila RTB, the psychotherapist, said if you want to stave off cognitive decline you should eat plenty of mushrooms. 'They contain something called ergothioneine, which is an antioxidant and anti-inflammatory substance that humans are unable to synthesise on their own,' she explained. No one ventured to argue with that.

Barbara, wife of a doctor, said that rubbing a raw onion on bee and wasp stings can break down the toxins and reduce any swelling.

Laila had advice for anyone suffering from haemorrhoids. 'You should stop eating peanuts and its derivatives, such as peanut butter and satay sauce, and see if it makes a difference,' she said. 'More people are allergic to peanuts than we realise, and they don't just cause swelling in the mouth and throat but at the other end of the body as well.' Who would have thought?

I often hear moans from my children about the difficulties of getting a doctor's appointment, especially with a child. A trivial but necessary consultation means missing a whole morning of school – and work for the accompanying parent – and bundling a sick child into the car and sitting for ages in a crowded waiting room is no fun either.

My children grew up in the 60s and 70s. There were no group practices then. A newly qualified GP would usually set up his surgery in his own home, the only recognition being a sign proclaiming his status in his front garden. One of the larger rooms would be the surgery where he saw his patients, with a few chairs in the hall for those awaiting his attention. His wife and children had to make do with the rest of the house.

Sometimes this overlapped, as with our family doctor, Dr Wilson, a delightful if somewhat overweight, chain-smoking saint who looked after all his patients as though they were members of his own family. Having said that, his method of making sure his patients only visited his home in a dire emergency was the other occupant of his house. No, not his wife or son but a HUGE Great Dane, easily seven-foot-high as demonstrated by his friendly greeting of putting his enormous paws on the patient's shoulders, leaving them quaking with terror. This was not assuaged by the reassurances of Mrs Wilson shouting from the kitchen, 'It's all right, he won't hurt you,' which soon put people at their ease – once they got up from the floor.

Having a dog contravened the Health Service hygiene laws and there was an official notice hanging on the wall of the 'waiting room' stipulating 'No Dogs allowed in the Surgery', under which Mrs Wilson had written, 'I prefer my dog to some of the patients' – but nobody objected.

A room intended as a dining room in a normal house was the surgery where Dr Wilson would sit behind an enormous desk piled with papers, samples of medications sent in vain by hopeful pharmaceutical companies, and so much other paraphernalia that it was difficult to see the patient sitting opposite. A skimpy curtain disguised the examination couch, covered with a clean, white sheet which I'm sure was scrupulously changed between each patient.

There was no apparent appointment system; you knew the surgery hour was 5pm till 6pm every evening and you just turned up and sat on the little chairs in his hall, chatting with the other patients until it was your turn. As the walls of his house were not soundproofed, snippets of conversations would occasionally drift through ('It can't be a sexually transmitted infection Doctor, I'm happily married!' or 'I have no idea how that got stuck up there') ensuring the whole neighbourhood was conversant with the medical history of all his patients.

Dr Wilson did not employ a receptionist, relying on local housewives (can I still use that word? But that's what they were then) to help out generally, like my sister, who worked there three mornings a week from 9 till 12, answering the phone and either handing the receiver to Dr Wilson or arranging for a home visit. In between, she would write out the prescriptions which he would sign. I assume she got the amounts right and, with practice, managed to fend off the daily greeting by the Great Dane sticking his nose in her crotch.

In between, Mrs Wilson, as all doctor's wives, would act as part-time nurse, receptionist, counsellor to the patients, and nag her husband about his health and peculiar dietary habits. Dr Wilson refused to eat anything that could 'swim or fly' – whether that included anything that could baa or moo was anyone's guess. His advice on healthy eating consisted of copious amounts of Mars bars and, strangely, strawberries.

If one of my kids was ill, the cry would go up, 'Call Dr Wilson', and a little while later the doorbell would ring and there he was with his scruffy bag full of magic tricks and air of calm authority. My husband would greet him in the time-honoured Jewish tradition: 'How's business?' to which he would reply, 'Business is good. Plenty of sick people around, thank God.'

He would be led to the room of the ailing child and proceed with the usual examination. Before looking in his small patient's ear, he would tell him, or her, to cover the other ear with their hand 'in case the light goes all the way through' and they would obey instantly. My son, now in his fifties, shamefacedly admits he still automatically does that when a doctor hoves in with his little torch thing, then quickly drops his hand.

Examination completed, the verbal prescription would usually be that the patient needed 'lots of chocolate, lots of television and should be able to go back to school tomorrow'.

Then, if he had time, a cup of tea 'would be nice, thank you' and a little chat about the current problems with the health service and the little six-year-old boy he saw yesterday whose listless appearance and other signs made him suspect the child might be diabetic. He had handed him a specimen jar and directed him towards his downstairs loo, saying 'I want you to do a little wee for me, OK?' The boy nodded and a few minutes later came out and handed the empty jar back to Dr Wilson saying, 'I didn't need that, there was a toilet in there.'

If the visit did reveal any worrying symptom, there was no referral to a specialist or prolonged wait in A & E. Dr Wilson would simply return that evening accompanied by a mate of his, some poor man he had probably dragged away from his dinner but who just happened to be a leading expert in that particular medical field, and the two men would perch on the young patient's bed and discuss the next step. And yes, whisky would be nice, thank you.

If any operation should be required, I know from personal experience that Dr Wilson would be in the actual operating theatre during the procedure and would appear afterwards, still gowned and masked, in the waiting room to reassure my worried husband and me that all was well. He would then advise us to take the patient home as soon as possible as 'a hospital is no place for sick people – too many germs.'

When my accident-prone son was about nine, he managed to put his leg through a glass door and I can still see in my mind this gentle, genial man sitting with his large bulk on my son's bed carefully picking bits of glass out of the boy's knee with tweezers and prescribing 'lots of chocolate, lots of television and back to school tomorrow'.

We were heartbroken when he died and North London lost one of the most brilliant characters ever produced by the National Health Service. They don't make them like that anymore.

This led us to compare the old-fashioned medical methods with today's standards which, in some ways, we found sadly lacking, particularly in relation to us older folks.

Jess was still complaining about her health and said she kept seeing a black, floaty thing at the front of her eye that moved when she did.

I said, 'Have you seen a doctor?' and she said, 'No only a black, floaty thing.'

Okaaay! More coffee anyone?

9

Is it just me??

There's an old story my dad used to tell about a proud mother watching her soldier son marching on parade during the war and saying to her friend, 'They're all out of step except my Johnnie.'

Well, that's how I feel sometimes, out of step with the normal populist viewpoint on so many things. Take holidays. I hate holidays. I can understand why people fancy a change sometimes. My friend Gloria goes on at least three cruises a year, and Sheila DTR can't wait to tie planks of wood to her feet and throw herself down the side of a snowy mountain as soon as winter approaches.

Me? Well, I haven't left the country in over twenty years and don't feel I've missed out on anything.

'You're just weird,' said Jess, as I decanted my usual lemon drizzle cake from the tin on to a plate – with a doily as my mother taught me. 'Everyone likes holidays. You need a break from everyday routine, and, by the way, can't you make anything other than lemon drizzle cake? You made that last time.'

I ignored her and said that I heard nowadays you have to fill in numerous forms and do a myriad of tests to ensure you are free of disease before you even set off. Then when you get to the airport you are strip-searched and they confiscate your moisturiser. In fact, I had to renew my passport recently and the previous one was completely empty, no stamps in it at all. So why bother to renew? Good question. I do it because you sometimes need a passport for official identification purposes.

The problem is I hate extremes of weather. I'm very uncomfortable being either too hot or too cold, which is why I live in England where these extreme weather conditions don't last longer than a few days. Therefore, it would make no sense for me to spend thousands of pounds to travel to a place and lie in blistering hot sun or sit and look at a pool all day. You also have to listen to the kind of conversations where mundane matters are elevated to vital importance by normally intelligent people when on holiday: 'What do you want to do about lunch?', 'Shall I book somewhere for tonight?', 'Are we meeting for drinks first?', 'Can we avoid that boozy couple from last night?'

I do realise there are other forms of holiday and, of course, I admire and appreciate stunning architecture, but when you've seen one Taj Mahal …

I realise I sound like a miserable cow but there are lots of things I really like: books – I'm never without a book on the go – I'm fascinated by people's stories; soul music; Cadbury's milk chocolate; exercise; musical theatre, blah blah. And I have it all right *here*. I believe that London is the culture capital of the world and I am so grateful that I live in a country where I am free to enjoy everything it has to offer. I'm pretty sure most people would disagree but I would honestly rather be in a theatre with my grandchildren watching Michael Ball in *Hairspray* – yet again! – than be stuck in a hotel where I have to find a café or order room service if I want a cup of tea. I know, totally weird.

I have no interest in fashion and hate shopping for clothes, living as I do in workout gear and trackie-bottoms, and consider well-cut jeans and a smart jacket 'dressing up'.

However, I can boast a connection with royalty as my mate, Camilla, Duchess of Cornwall gets her shoes from the same supplier as I do, *Sole Bliss*, as we share a tendency for bunions (she has admitted this before) and these shoes are a Godsend as they are specially made for people similarly afflicted. Although, having said that, I have one pair of black court shoes for winter and a beige pair for summer and that's it, so maybe Camilla beats me on numbers. She's never confided.

This sort of mindset means that I am the worst kind of mother my son Gary could have chosen, as he is a jeweller and I have no interest in watches, bracelets or anything I have to fiddle with in my ears or round my neck. I do understand that discreet pieces of jewellery can add glamour to an outfit, but bloody great chandeliers or huge hoops hanging from a woman's ears do her no favours at all, in my opinion. My diamond engagement ring was stolen by a former nanny and I never replaced my wedding ring when it got bent out of shape after I dropped it down the waste-disposal unit.

Gary left school at 16 and joined a prestigious top-class – i.e. expensive – jewellery company, starting in the workroom learning about all the different stones and how to design and make the various pieces to be sold in the shop. He made me a lovely ring with – what's that blue stone called? – for my 40th birthday which I still wear with pride whenever I remember to put it back on again after washing my hands.

Having been in the trade for forty years, Gary is now an expert in diamonds and, working from his lair in Hatton Garden, specialises in designing and making beautiful engagement rings for a fraction of the price of buying the same item in a shop.

Then there are watches. People collect watches. Why? I guess it's a hobby like any other, but when did a watch become more than a gadget to tell the time? I don't get it. And it's not any old watch that collectors want but the latest one of a certain make. Gary told me that someone wanting the latest Patek Philippe watch could wait seven years before acquiring it if they didn't get on the waiting list fast enough. Really? Apparently, a Daytona Rolex (this is Gary talking – that could be a washing machine for all I know!) is available at four times the retail price – if you are willing to wait two years.

This is obviously way beyond my comprehension. But don't get me wrong, I'm absolutely not judging anyone here. Everyone can do whatever they like, *I'm* the one who is out of sync with the rest of the world. My sister, who is the direct opposite of me in every way, apart from a love of family and a sense of humour that binds us tightly together, loves jewellery. Besides being beautiful, stylish, and up-to-date fashion-wise, she never goes out without her ears and wrists adorned with a neat and beautiful piece

– and that makes her happy. She also always beats me at Scrabble which is very annoying.

And what's with handbags? Even I can understand that an expensive diamond watch is a luxury item, but a handbag? Some women put their names on a waiting list for a designer handbag costing thousands of pounds which won't be in their possession till the season after the season after that. Again, why? Obviously, they must love the bag very much and that's fine. I just can't understand why they bother. It can't be to impress a man. I have never heard a man say, 'Wow, you look fantastic carrying that handbag'.

Another 'out-of-step-Johnnie' confession: I have one 'good' black handbag, which was given to me as a birthday present 17 years ago, that I use when I go out anywhere smart. (It's probably got an old sixpence tucked into the lining!) Apart from that, I buy a new 'everyday' bag from Marks when the old one falls apart. But hey, if you crave a handbag that you really love and not just because you've seen a picture of Victoria Beckham holding it, then good for you – enjoy using something that gives you pleasure.

According to a recent report, owning top-of-the-range handbags, watches and shoes (shoes?) have to be factored in when the joint finances are divided in a divorce settlement. Seriously. The courts are required to step in when couples cannot agree who would keep assets such as a Hermès handbag, Rolex watches or Louboutin shoes. And I thought the most important items discussed in a divorce case were who has custody of the kids …

According to an analysis of 'investments of passion' (oh please!) by estate agents Knight Frank, handbags were the designer item that rose most in value during the Covid lockdown, with Hermès leading the trend, up 17 per cent. There is even something called The Handbag Clinic, where an 'expert' will authenticate and value designer bags – similar, I guess, to verifying the artist of a famous painting. This is presumably to differentiate between your £6,000 Chanel Classic and a similar 'Channel' bag your friend bought from a guy on the beach in Marbella for a fiver.

The most bizarre latest trend for me is women collecting designer carrier bags. Yes, you read it right – you just *have* to be seen clutching an array of carrier bags bearing names like Lanvin, Cartier, Chloé and Celine, dahling. Do they contain items from those stores? No, but who cares if they add a bit of wishful thinking and a little lustre to your life. But what gets me is that these carrier bags are being sold online for hundreds of pounds. Not the possible contents of even a much-desired secondhand Hermès Birkin but the packaging they are sold in – with the most coveted being those iconic black-and-white Chanel carriers. A collection of 17 reportedly sold for £265!

People who can't afford the expensive watches acquired for customers by my son Gary are buying the empty boxes on eBay. For example, a Rolex box would go for £160. What do they do with these boxes? Wear them on their wrists?

I wish I had kept my empty boxes when I bought trainers in the past because, according to the website *money.co.uk*, even I could have got £55 for the *box* containing my Nikes! People are even buying *empty* scented candle jars and perfume bottles, which would start at £50 if they're by Diptyque or Saint Laurent. Who is buying this stuff? Certainly not anyone I know. Or maybe they are, and that lady in my reading group has painted the soles of her shoes red to persuade everyone they are Louboutins. Who knows?

As for me, I just don't get it!

10

Let's have a clear-out

Like everyone else trapped in their homes during the lockdown due to the Covid pandemic in 2020, I looked around and despaired of the amount of stuff cluttering up every shelf, cupboard and drawer in my house. There is a small area just off my kitchen where Pete, my builder, erected a unit comprising of shelves almost to the ceiling and two cupboards at the base. The shelves are packed with games I play with my grandchildren, recipe books I never look at, box files containing goodness knows what, and, inexplicably, bottles of wine. I don't drink.

Again, like a lot of people during this enforced incarceration, I decided to have a clear-out and get rid of any surplus junk, and may even have made a start before realising that the municipal tip was closed, so that took care of that.

However, when I opened a hall cupboard and a box of my late husband's old hats fell off a shelf and, in doing so, knocked the vacuum cleaner so that it toppled and hit my forehead, I decided enough was enough. I was going to have a clear-out.

As always, I dragged my friend Nancy along to help and support me in my endeavour on the basis that someone else's possessions are much more interesting than your own. And also promising to give her a slice of lemon drizzle cake to take home. We decided we were going to be very efficient about this and sat down in the kitchen to 'Make a Plan'.

In a pristine notebook we put headings:

Allotted time per session: Obviously we weren't going to get the whole house done in one day so we decided not to work longer than two hours at any one time in case we got fed up and abandoned the whole idea.

Things we need:
- Several strong plastic tubs of various sizes, some with lids
- Strong black bin bags
- Cardboard boxes from the supermarket to cart stuff to the tip
- Rubber gloves
- Cleaning materials, sprays and sponges.
- One packet of chocolate Hobnobs

De-cluttering Rules: We decided to divide all objects into four categories: Keep – Sell on eBay – Charity shop – Chuck out.

We were very satisfied with the professional way we were going about this task and decided that was enough for one day so we settled down to watch *Countdown*. Nancy, who is a whizz at crosswords, got the nine-letter conundrum immediately, which was very irritating.

The following day, Nancy turned up already wearing rubber gloves and brandishing a toilet plunger for some reason, although my plumbing is perfectly intact. We decided to start with the attic and I told Nancy to go ahead of me, rather like sending a canary down a coalmine (today's youngsters wouldn't have a clue what I was talking about!) in case there were any spiderwebs – or their occupants.

Nancy said she will never forget her son's scream of terror when he entered her attic to retrieve his school reports and came upon his great-grandmother's fox fur stole, complete with head and claws, which had somehow escaped from the disintegrating carrier bag that contained it. Nancy said she had been meaning to sell it for years but had discovered that nobody wanted to buy it. Strange, that.

The dim light bulb in my attic revealed an area packed with old heavy suitcases, boxes of papers, a mattress, chest of drawers, filing cabinet and a mass of other sundries.

'Good grief!' Nancy said. 'There's more furniture in here than in my combined dining/living rooms.'

I explained that my children assumed my house was some sort of free storage facility and all this stuff was there 'in case' – meaning that armchair that opened into a bed might be useful 'in case' someone came to stay at my daughter's house. I assumed she'd forgotten about it along with the boxes of baby clothes from her now 17-year-old daughter. Was this 'in case' she was thinking of having another baby? At 57 it's unlikely!

Ooh look, there's my old rocking horse, Walter, that I used to ride as a child and imagine I was galloping along the prairie, chasing baddies with my trusty sidekick, Hopalong Cassidy (remember him, Reader?). Walter has been through five generations and several cousins. How could I send him to the knacker's yard?

I opened a box containing an old portable television, two cassette players, amplifiers, VHS machines, speakers, TV remotes and hundreds of cables once connecting God-knows-what. Then shut it again.

We decided the attic wasn't a good place to start, as the owners of those items would have to decide for themselves what to do with them and Nancy and I weren't exactly built for lifting furniture. So that was enough for today and we settled down to watch *The Chase* because we love Bradley Walsh and congratulated each other by high-fiving when we got an obvious question right and echoing his phrase 'All-day-long'.

The following week, Nancy dragged me into my bedroom and decided we were going to sort out my clothes. She declared herself an expert at de-cluttering having watched two episodes of Marie Kondo on YouTube.

I climbed on a chair and retrieved a box from a top cupboard filled with clothes 'in case' I wanted to wear them again.

'What on earth's this?' Nancy declared, pulling out a green satin evening dress.

'I wore that for my sister's wedding,' I protested. 'I'm sure it still fits me.'

'When did your sister get married?'

'I think it was 1964.'

She held it up. 'And you think your waist might magically reappear or you can turn up in public in a low-cut dress without wearing a bra? Get real, girl! In the charity box it goes.'

Other items followed suit, most of which I didn't even recognise. Purple velvet hotpants anyone? Moi? Oh yes, in the 70s with a long pink T-shirt and a belt slung low on my hips. I was one cool chick, I can tell you!

In the charity box.

Nancy opened my T-shirt drawer. 'Leave it' I said. 'I know what I've got and I'm happy with the way it looks now.'

'No no,' Nancy protested. 'Marie Kondo says you don't just pile T-shirts on top of each other, even if they are folded nicely. You have to roll each one up then fold it into a little bundle and place each one neatly side by side in a single layer in the drawer. Then you can see all of them without rummaging.'

'But with that method, how do you know if a T-shirt has long or short sleeves or is a V-neck or round neck?' I asked.

'You'd have to pull each one out and check,' she said. I see.

We looked at the small pile of clothes ready for the charity shop and decided that was a good result for one day and settled down to watch the aptly named *Pointless Celebrities*. We amused ourselves by counting how many times Alexander Armstrong uttered his buying-time phrase, 'thank you very much *in-deed*!' in one hour's programme. Once I counted him saying it over 30 times.

Nancy went on holiday after that so we left it for a few weeks. On her return, we pledged to return to our task and decided to tackle the cupboard in the spare room. This turned out to contain spare duvets, pillows and covers for both, towels and sheets. They were all in reasonably good condition so we put them all back.

Nancy then spied a cardboard box at the back and pulled it out. It was full to the brim of old photos dating back to the last century.

'That's me as a little girl,' I said, noticing Nancy holding a picture of a peculiar-looking child screwing up her face.

'I didn't know you had curly, frizzy hair!' she said.

Aha! What would I do without my weekly blow-dry with the handsome stylist, James, and the liberal use of my GHD straightening irons in between to ensure my fringe lies flat instead of a mass of frizz? I dread to think. (She didn't know I had grey hair either!)

Nancy and I decided we'd done enough clearing out for now and settled down happily to look through the photos, with a plate of the aforementioned chocolate Hobnobs in front of us and *Tipping Point* playing on the television in the background.

11

Author! Author?

My friend Barbara was thrilled to bits. We are both members of our local branch of the University of Third Age (U3A) and join seven other women in the weekly Creative Writing Course run by a wonderful former journalist, Sue, who used to write for various publications, including the *Observer* newspaper and *Woman's Weekly* magazine.

As one of our exercises, Barbara wrote a charming piece featuring herself as a small child getting lost on a beach and she announced that it had been accepted for publication in *The Oldie* magazine. For amateur writers this is a huge achievement when you consider how many people think of themselves as authors and continually send stuff in to magazines, usually in vain.

We all gave Barbara a round of applause and broke open a carton of green top for tea with the cherry Bakewell tart she had made and brought along to celebrate the start of her literary career. I thought the cake was a bit stodgy at first so I had to have a larger second slice just to confirm my diagnosis, and I was right, it was a bit stodgy. Whoever cut it had done so at an angle so it looked uneven, which irritated me, so I had to pick up the knife and cut another small slice to 'tidy it up'.

Sue-the-journalist encouraged each of us to write a memoir to hand down to our grandchildren and to be passed to future generations. 'You might think your life is mundane,' she said, 'but your great-great-grandchildren will be fascinated by your experiences. For example, how you laid flowers at Kensington Palace when King William's mother died, and how you used to drive a 'car'. On the road! They won't believe it.'

We all looked a bit dubious but agreed it was a nice idea. I trimmed a bit more of the cake and popped the 'trimmings' into my mouth until I was satisfied the remaining cake formed a perfect 45 degree angle. Barbara said I could take the rest of it home if I liked, but I declined, saying it was too stodgy.

I was the only one of the group who had actually had a book published. Even so, I continued to attend the meeting each week because you can always learn about your craft. Having said that, having a book published is very exciting. It's a feeling of elation mixed with a certain amount of trepidation when you first hold the actual printed tome in your hands. Did I really write this? Suppose nobody buys it?

Ah, that's the crux: how to, firstly, get it into the shops and, secondly, persuade enough people to buy it and spread the word so that more people buy it. This generates something called royalties, a monetary reward being a percentage of the sales paid to the author once all the people involved in the production have taken their cut. Unless your name is J K Rowling or Richard Osman, I wouldn't advise anyone to count on this as a way of earning a living.

My book, *Getting Old, Deal with It*, was officially published in January, 2020. Before that actual date, the amazingly efficient publicity lady, Ruth, part of Team Mensch Publishing, put the word out to all her contacts in the media that this extremely funny, informative book was about to be launched and would they please get back to her with dates for interviews.

They did. A wonderful double-page spread appeared in a Sunday magazine which started the ball rolling, then my diary was filled with interviews with the likes of Talk Radio, Steve Wright at the BBC, Irish National Radio, and so on.

I absolutely hated doing them – hated it! I know, I know, most authors would give their eye teeth for the chance to chat about their book. My problem is that when I have finished doing something – seeing a play, reading a book … indeed, *writing* a book – I forget about it and move on to the next thing. I also have a large family that needs my attention and I still work as a fitness instructor, so I don't really focus on past achievements.

Therefore, between the time I finished writing my book, which was March 2019, and the date it actually appeared in the bookshops the following January, after going through the process of approving a cover design and tormenting my poor editor for the best part of a year, I had forgotten most of what I'd written.

So when someone in my exercise class bounded up to me and said, 'I loved your book, especially that bit about your mother and her make-up routine,' I truly couldn't remember what she was referring to. That did not bode well during interviews when you are meant to chat seamlessly about the contents and deflect any questions you don't like with the dexterity of a politician.

I couldn't do this. Even though I'd prepared some notes, I stammered and stuttered and mumbled, then my mind went blank. For instance, the obvious question an interviewer would ask is, 'Why did you write this book?' and my truthful answer would be, 'I've no idea'. Not helpful. 'What's your book about?' Um, I don't remember.

It reminded me of the book launch for the autobiography written by the model, Naomi Campbell. When asked what her book was about she said, 'I don't know, I haven't read it yet.'

You can imagine, then, my terror when the uber-efficient Ruth-the-publicity-lady emailed to say I was to appear in the ITV programme, *This Morning*, hosted by the husband and wife team, Eamonn Holmes and Ruth Langsford. Gulp! Live TV. Live! All the possible screw-ups happening then and there, no editing, no patient book editor emailing 'You can't write that!' eight months before the public set eyes on your work. Camera, action, you're on! Oh God!

'Don't worry,' emailed Ruth, 'they're very nice and very experienced, you'll be fine.'

A date was set for a Friday in January. My initial thought was regretting all the mince pies I had indulged in over Christmas and, knowing the camera adds at least 10lbs, vowed to cut out all carbs from now till then. I was just wondering what to wear for my star appearance when I had a phone call from a nice young man from ITV. He said he needed to ask me some standard questions before my appearance. I said OK – (quick, quick, think of something: why did I write the book?)

He said, 'Have you ever been arrested?' What?! No. 'Well, do you have any criminal convictions?' No, of course not, have I been booked to appear on *Crimewatch* by mistake? Next question: 'Do you have any mental health problems?' By now, I'm beginning to wonder. Nooo. He sensed my hesitation and assured me these were standard questions he had to ask everyone. Next? 'Have you ever taken part in any pornographic films?' Surely this is a wind-up! Is he aware of my age? I couldn't resist saying, 'Not yet, but you never know.'

He explained that even though the show doesn't go out until 10.30, a car would collect me at 6.30 am (6.30?!) as I would need to have my hair and make-up done and a rehearsal beforehand. A rehearsal? Oh yes, I would be demonstrating some exercises suitable for older people and Eamonn and Ruth may join in. Oh my Lord, that meant I would be appearing on live television in workout gear. As if I wasn't stressed enough!

I asked who else would be on the show and he said the singer Tom Jones. Tom Jones – I love Tom Jones! I excitedly emailed my daughter – guess who? She came back with, 'Oh, your favourite, you must get a selfie with him.'

The date imprinted itself in my mind as the days went by – and the nights where I lay awake trying to think of some witty answers. I practised some flexibility exercises that might be suitable for beginners and packed a small bag with a selection of clothes for the experts to advise me what would work best for the camera.

The day before the big Friday another researcher tele-phoned me to check everything was OK for the following day. I assured him it was. I planned to set my alarm for 5.30am and vowed to have an early night, hoping to banish the residual bags under my eyes by the morning.

At 4pm, that same day, there was another call from the researcher. 'I've just come out of a production meeting,' he said, 'and I'm afraid we have to cancel your appearance tomorrow. There's some breaking story they have to deal with. I'm really sorry but this happens all the time in TV – I'm sure you understand.'

Oh. OK. I felt a combination of relief and slight dis-appointment. I'm not going to be a TV star after all. I'm not going to meet Tom Jones. Oh well. I reset my alarm for the usual wake-up time and slept soundly that night for the first time in weeks.

I dreamt I sang a duet with Tom Jones. I suppose it's not unusual.

12

Mind over matter (if you don't mind, it doesn't matter)

Last Wednesday, my group of friends and I all met at Gloria's house – well, at one of them. She owns several, including a house in London, a flat in Spain and a villa in Miami, where she resides from January to April to escape the British winter. I don't think I've mentioned Gloria much in these pages as we don't see her very often for the reason just stated.

In spite of living in various countries, Gloria has managed to collect a vast array of grandchildren. She only actually gave birth to three children, but they all married in haste, divorced in haste and remarried even more hastily – sometimes more than once. Every time one of these transactions took place, they added a gaggle of stepchildren to their brood, each one clasped to Gloria's ample bosom and claimed as an additional grandchild. She loved them all.

In fact, she had been known to drag a young grandson, who had fallen and was covered in mud and dog poo, up the stairs, stripped off his clothes and plonked him in a bath. Once the child was de-mudded she found herself gazing at a complete stranger, who was probably wondering how he came to find himself sitting in a mud-stained bath, in a strange house with some mad woman.

As the years went by she forgot which ones were biologically hers and, seemingly, so did they, when as teenagers and twenty-year-olds they would turn up at one of her homes usually with a gang of their step-sibs or friends – she was never sure which – and she would claim them too.

Once our Wednesday group were all gathered at Gloria's house – the one in London – she declared she was on a diet. Because of this, she had forgone baking her usual apricot-surprise cake – so called because on one occasion she forgot to add the apricots – and had substituted cut-up carrots, cucumber and red peppers (not in the cake) with a variety of dips.

The only person unhappy with this was Deely who grumbled that this was supposed to be a 'coffee 'n' cake' meeting not 'coffee 'n' celery'. Jess replied tartly that it wouldn't do Deely any harm to join Gloria in losing a few pounds. Deely agreed. 'I wish everything was as easy as putting *on* weight. Maybe it would help if I started putting milk on my Weetabix instead of Baileys.'

'You should come and stay with me in Miami,' said Gloria. 'The complex where I live organises an exercise session every morning in the courtyard and all the old people are encouraged to join in.'

'I wish,' said Deely, and sighed. 'I haven't managed to get to the gym again this week. That's three years in a row.'

Then Pauline announced loudly, 'I think I've got dementia.'

She explained that after fifteen months of being too terrified to leave her house during the enforced lockdown due to the Covid pandemic, she ventured out to her local supermarket to do a big shop. At the checkout she discovered, to her horror, that she had forgotten the 4-digit PIN for her credit card. 'I started shaking,' she said. 'That number has been engraved in my brain for ever and I've never had a problem with it before. My mind was blank. Luckily, I had enough cash on me to pay and, once I was in the car, the number popped back in my mind again. Scary. That's the start of dementia, isn't it?'

'You haven't got dementia,' declared Sheila RTB, the psychotherapist. 'If you *think* you have, that means you *haven't* got it because if you really had it you wouldn't be able to think you've got it.' So that's cleared that up then.

'So I must have Long Covid,' said Pauline. 'You know, brain fog and all that.'

'But you haven't had Short Covid,' Barbara reminded her.

'Well, who knows what those antibodies they injected into me are doing?' said Pauline, refusing to give up. 'I'm still suffering from postnatal depression.'

'Oh come on! How old is your Jamie?'

'54.'

We all thought we were going mad during the lockdown, especially us older folk. The message was loud and clear: 'Stay in your house, old person. If you so much as go near another person you will die!' No wonder it scared the bejesus out of us …

We are all so independent and determined not to be a nuisance to our children, and here we were, being a nuisance to our children, although they didn't see it that way. 'Send me your shopping list,' texted my son – or he meant to, but as he put 'shipping list' I couldn't resist ordering a canoe, a tanker and a submarine.

We tried keeping in touch with each other by Zoom, with the inevitable resulting mayhem:

'I can't see you'

'Well I can see you, but I can't hear you'

'Who's that in the corner of the screen?'

'What?'

'You've disappeared!'

'No, you've cut me off!'

So it was back to the old telephone, text and email system, which kept us going until the restrictions eased. We were particularly worried about Sheila DTR who professed to have a huge crush on Professor Chris Whitty, the Chief Medical Officer of the Government's Scientific Advisory Group for Emergencies (SAGE) and tuned in eagerly to watch him on every news bulletin. 'I love his way with graphs,' she said. 'I just want to straighten his tie and give him a big hug. Don't you?' Er, no.

We agreed we all lose our keys occasionally and wonder why we opened the fridge. Personally, I'm happy when I go upstairs and remember what I went up there for.

'It's quite common to go into a room for something, then get distracted and come back without it,' explained Sheila. 'In psychiatric terms it's called the "doorway effect". When you go in or out of a room through a doorway, that becomes a sort of boundary in your mind and makes your brain believe a new scene has begun and that you don't need to remember the old scene. We remember things by association, which is why you have to retrace your steps to what happened before you went through the door.'

That sounded plausible. 'It won't be a problem for me,' said Pauline. 'The way my memory is going, I'll end up in one room anyway.'

We decided to have a little quiz to test all our memories. At the time of writing there is a revival of the 1930s musical 'Anything Goes' playing at a London theatre, with music by the wonderful composer Cole Porter. I Googled some more of his songs, and we all wrote down ten titles:

1 Anything Goes
2 Don't Fence Me In
3 Too Darn Hot
4 I've Got You Under my Skin
5 Miss Otis Regrets
6 I Get a Kick out of You
7 Let's Do It, Let's Fall in Love
8 All of Me
9 Begin the Beguine
10 Every Time We Say Goodbye

'Right,' I said (I can be really bossy at times), 'you've got two minutes to look at those titles, then we're going to turn the paper over and see how many we can remember.'

I was quite proud of myself for getting nine titles right out of the ten. I don't know how many the others got because Sheila got distracted by a text, Jess grumbled that the room was too hot, Deely stood up to get some carrot sticks and tripped over the rug, and the others kept singing 'A Nightingale Sang in Berkeley Square' which was written by someone else entirely. (I checked and it was composed by Manning Sherwin. Me neither.)

I guess we'll all have to go along with Nietzsche's philosophy, which is 'the advantage of a bad memory is it enables you to enjoy several times the same good things for the first time'.

More celery anyone?

13

Putting the 'fun' in funerals

Some years ago, I joined the meagre crowd attending the funeral of my uncle Henry, formerly Heinrich, and listened to the Rabbi reciting a list of all his virtues whilst not recognising any of them.

Uncle Henry was a cantankerous old bugger who had cheated death for 91 years and was thoroughly disliked by everyone who came in contact with him. His wife and only son emigrated to New Zealand years ago, presumably to get as far away from him as possible. Neither came to the funeral.

The only other relative in attendance was his older sister, my aunt Dora, who was the exact opposite of her horrible brother and spent a lot of time placating the wonderfully patient staff in the care home where he lived. He would swear at them in German and be unpleasant to all the other residents. They must be having a celebratory wake there this evening.

Dora was a sprightly 96-year-old with all her marbles intact and a wicked sense of humour which I modestly hope I've inherited. As we stood at the graveside, she looked around and said, 'I don't know if it's worth my going home.' We made each other laugh on the journey home by imagining what she would engrave on his tombstone, suggestions being 'To know him was to dislike him' and 'He will be gladly missed'.

I was thinking of this when, at a charity dinner, I found myself sitting (not 'sat') next to a charming man named Gerry who turned out to be a retired funeral director. You don't meet one of those every day of the week!

He told me his field of expertise included arranging both traditional burials and cremations, so I took the opportunity to ask if he had officiated at any unusual ceremonies. He said that, although the limousines and black hearses were the norm, some people liked to arrive in style in the old fashioned carriage and horses, complete with two coachmen in traditional top hats sitting on top. We've all been in a traffic jam behind one of those. He had also had requests for a fire engine and a London bus.

Being a traditionalist, Gerry hated having to witness the habit of sending the ashes up in a firework display or having a crowd of friends or relatives turn up to a funeral wearing their local team's football shirts with a photo of the deceased pinned to the back. He also used to get irritated when a family and numerous relatives arrived for a funeral complete with an entire film crew to record the event for a memorial video. He had to put up with lighting, sound checks and fully expected to hear, 'Could you do that bit again, mate, we didn't quite catch that'. This was obviously before the online funerals necessary during the Covid pandemic lockdown rules, which at least meant people could attend safely.

And of course there are the songs. Gerry groaned when I mentioned music. 'Why?' he said. 'Why must they do this?

Is it to make people cry? I've never understood it, especially as the sound system is – shall we be blunt and say – crap at most of these places and sometimes people have to stop themselves laughing inappropriately rather than be moved when the music wavers all over the place. He mentioned one occasion when relatives played the deceased's favourite concerto which went on for about fifteen minutes, causing restlessness amongst those members of the congregation not conversant with the classical genre and irritation from the officials aware of the waiting room filling up with mourners for the next funeral.

Gerry would have been horrified at the last online funeral I attended when one music track was greeted with rapturous applause at the end of the recording – not appropriate at all!

I was interested, though, and persuaded Gerry to give me a few of the favourite songs played at funerals. First choice evidently is *My Way* by Frank Sinatra, followed by *Wind Beneath My Wings* by Bette Midler. Robbie Williams' *Angels* is increasingly played, but a firm favourite is – predictably – *Time to Say Goodbye* by Andrea Bocelli and Sarah Brightman. Actually, I think *Softly, as I Leave You* by Matt Monro would really start me off.

I decided to ask my Wednesday group what songs they would like played at their funeral. We were meeting at the home of Sheila DTR so I didn't have far to go. It just so happened that this day was a Jewish festival called Purim and she had baked some pastries called *hamantaschen* which are traditionally eaten on this occasion. They are triangular-shaped pastries filled with poppy seeds. I'm not sure what they are meant to represent, but Laila, who is Muslim, loved them. Me, not so much, as the poppy seeds stuck in my teeth.

However, as the first song title suggestion was *Another One Bites the Dust* by Queen, I abandoned that idea and we started discussing whether we would want to be buried or cremated. Or neither, as Barbara said she intended to live to 120 and book herself on a continuous round-the-world cruise, and when she died they could throw her overboard.

I told them that Gerry mentioned people requesting their ashes be sent up in a firework display and that I didn't believe that, but Laila said she read in the press that the business genius, Sir Terence Conran, who died in September 2020 had left definite instructions that his ashes should be sent into the sky and exploded in a fireworks display at his Berkshire home accompanied by a playing of Handel's firework music. I hope he got his wish.

Sheila said she saw an article about the price of coffins having risen sharply over the last decade and that there was actually a website called *Comparethecoffin.com* to help you choose one.

'That's the last thing I need!' said Jess. I told you she had a sense of humour.

This invariably led to what we would want engraved on our tombstones when the time came. Again, I should have thought twice before bringing up the subject as someone immediately spouted the old inscription used by Spike Milligan: 'I told you I was ill.'

That started them off:

'She made the best Yorkshire puddings.'

'I knew this would happen!'

'I wanted a pyramid.'

'Which pedal is the brake again?'

'This isn't funny, let me out NOW!'

Deely said to me, 'I'll write your obituary if you like'

I said indignantly, 'Over my dead body!'

14

A jive down memory lane

We were having a disagreement about the correct way to pronounce the word 'scones' which Nancy had inadvertently started when she produced a plate of these instead of the usual cake. Barbara said they should rhyme with 'cons' while Laila, who has lived in the UK a mere 50 years, insisted they should rhyme with 'crones'. It appeared that those of us who grew up in London preferred the latter version, whilst those who gravitated to the capital from elsewhere favoured the former.

The argument – sorry, discussion – then turned to whether it was appropriate to add the cream to a cut scone first, or the jam – and whether this should be strawberry or raspberry. Plain scones or with raisins. This will give you some idea of the philosophical and intellectual nature of our discourses. Personally, as long as my scone was slathered in salted butter I didn't care how it was pronounced.

The talk then turned to grandchildren and their obsession with their mobile phones. Four of my granddaughters are teenagers and their mothers complain constantly about how difficult it is to get them away from their mobile phones. There are reports that children are actually showing symptoms of stress when parted from their devices for any length of time.

This is difficult to understand for my generation, especially the behaviour that is generated by owning one of these wretched things. My friends and I reluctantly had to acquire a mobile phone because we couldn't park our cars without the Pay-by-Phone app. We gradually got used to the convenience of texting or phoning a friend to say, 'I've been in the pub for twenty minutes, where are you?'

However, we do not post pouty pictures of ourselves in bikinis doing an inverted yoga pose, nor do we gauge our popularity by the number of positive responses we get to this. I've read that in schools, the practice of 'upskirting', where a boy will take pictures up a girl's skirt on his phone and circulate them to his friends is now illegal. If a boy wanted to do that in my schooldays, he would have to lie on the floor with a Polaroid camera which would require the consent of all participants.

This led to thoughts of my own teenage years. I was born in 1939 and would therefore become a 'teenager' in the early 50s which was when the word was invented due to the large numbers of kids in that age bracket. The music we loved was traditional jazz and the dance was jive. To get anywhere in the dating world you had to be able to jive and we would practise with each other at school so as to be proficient when asked to dance at the 'socials' held in church halls on a Saturday night. I wonder if the boys did the same thing as they mostly had to stand and jiggle whilst leading the girl as she twirled and flick-kicked.

Girls actually waited to be asked to dance at these events, with youth leaders from the church urging 'everyone on the floor', and the five-piece jazz band hired for the occasion would strike up with '*South Rampart Street Parade*'. You usually sat with your best friend and waited until a boy stood before you and jerked his head towards the moving throng, which was a signal for you to join him on the floor. If your friend was asked to dance and you weren't, you might nonchalantly wander to the ladies' toilet and wait there for a while so as not to be thought unpopular. There was no alcohol, the most daring drink being Coca-Cola.

If you danced more than once with a boy, especially if it was a slow, smoochy song, he could ask for your telephone number and promise to phone you, which would cause much giggling and speculation with your girlfriends later.

We watched films like *Some Like it Hot* and *High Society* which featured the wonderful Louis Armstrong playing the music we loved. Our parents were very protective and would take us to the dance venue and embarrass us by coming inside to check there was no alcohol being served, then issue instructions that we should be ready and waiting outside to be collected at 10pm, no later. The only activity not supervised was when my friend Sandra and I were allowed to go ice-skating at Queens Skating Rink in London. They thought we'd be perfectly safe there – and I'm sure we would have been – if we had actually gone there!

Yes, every Sunday afternoon, Sandra and I would leave our houses with ten shillings (50p) in our pockets and our pristine white ice-skating boots slung over our shoulders, tied together by their laces. The money would cover our bus fare to the tube station – about tuppence halfpenny – the train fare to Queensway, and entry to the rink. It would also cover a drink in the interval and the return journey.

What our parents didn't know, however, is that we didn't go to Queensway but stopped off at Leicester Square and made our way to 41 Windmill Street, just opposite the Windmill Theatre, and down the steps to the glorious haven of the Cy Laurie Jazz Club.

It was actually a total dump with a few dilapidated sofas round the room and a clapped out sound-system, but the atmosphere was electric as couples jived to the traditional jazz of clarinettist, Cy Laurie, and his six-piece band. After paying our three shillings (20p?) to get in, Sandra and I parked our skates in the dingy cloakroom and jived to our hearts' content all afternoon to the strains of *Muskrat Ramble* and *When the Saints Go Marching In*. Refreshments were limited to soft drinks and crisps dispensed from a crude bar, next to equally crude toilets, and although the musicians probably took drugs, I was never aware that anyone else did.

There were other popular traditional jazz clubs at this time. Some of my friends, freer from parental scrutiny, would make their way to trumpeter Humphrey Lyttleton's club at 100 Oxford Street, known as 'Humphs', where the same great music would waft into the street – rather like our own mini New Orleans. Bands like Chris Barber, Acker Bilk and Kenny Ball even had hits in the Top Ten music charts.

Alternative bands emerged at roughly the same time with another group of musicians forming a jazz band around the tenor sax player Ronnie Scott, who also opened his own club. They played modern jazz and would have nothing to do with 'trad' jazz which they considered an anachronism, with aficionados of each group looking down on the other as inferior. Modern jazz was considered 'pure', but who could jive to a saxophone meandering up and down a scale? Not me and my friends.

Cy Laurie himself wasn't always there on those Sunday afternoons. That period was regarded as a jam session when any competent, amateur musician with a penchant for trad jazz could turn up and play with the band. Two of my friends, Colin and Keith, played trumpet and clarinet respectively, which added another layer of security should I need it. But there was never any trouble. I loved every minute, and my parents didn't suspect a thing as I arrived home glowing and happy from my 'skating' exertions.

Gradually, as the 50s progressed, the type of music changed and when Bill Haley invited us to *Rock Around the Clock* we jived to that too, as with Little Richard's *Lucille* and Jerry Lee Lewis's *Great Balls of Fire*. Eventually though, even our dancing style changed and when Chubby Checker told us to '*Twist Again, Like We Did Last Summer*' we did that too!

From what I can see, kids today don't actually dance. The dance groups like Diversity, performing highly energetic, stylised routines, are incredible to watch and the moves are copied by teenagers, but how do boys and girls get to meet each other? Oh yes, dating apps!

15

Dating is definitely not a game!

'Do you know any nice girls for my Jason?' asked Nancy as we finished our game of Scrabble (she won) and the object of her adoration came into the room.

'Don't start, Mum,' he said, crossly, giving her a look I recognised only too well from my own children. 'I'm quite capable of finding my own women.'

He stomped out of the room and I asked Nancy what happened to the lovely girl he had been dating?

'Trina dumped him,' she said sadly, 'which is a shame because I really thought they could make a go of it. He's been living here for the past two weeks until he can find a place of his own.'

I've known Jason since before he was born and was aware that he and his wife, the mother of Nancy's two grown-up grandchildren, divorced more than ten years ago. He moved in with Trina four years ago and we all thought that would be permanent.

'He's joined all these match-making apps,' said Nancy, 'but I don't think it's going too well.'

'How old is Jason now?' I asked.

'In his late 40s.'

'How late?'

'51.'

'So is he looking for some glamorous 25-year-old?' I asked, but at that moment the suitor himself came back into the room. I asked him to explain how this dating app arrangement worked and he sighed.

'No, I don't want some young air-head bimbo,' he said, having overheard my comment. 'I'm looking for a nice, normal woman in her forties, someone you can have a decent conversation with and who is reasonably attractive. I wouldn't go for anyone with tattoos or a nose-ring or with too much junk in the trunk.'

With what?

'He means a fat bum,' explained Nancy. 'It's my fault, like everything else. I've always been slim so, even though a girl can be absolutely lovely, he won't date her if she's even a bit overweight.'

I gave him a disapproving look and he gave a 'what can I do?' shrug.

He flicked through his phone and showed me some pictures of women from the dating app he had joined. Each one was gorgeous. What's the problem?

'They lie,' he said. 'They lie on their profiles, sometimes knocking five years off their ages, and those pictures are often years out of date.'

'Don't the men lie as well?' I asked, and he said, 'Probably. The photos might be doctored to hide bald patches or a beer gut. But all these sites are favourable to women. If they like your picture, they make the first move and you have to respond within 24 hours. That can develop into a text-chat and eventually to a face-to-face meeting, which can lead to one of four outcomes: 1) You both like each other, 2) You like her but she doesn't like you, 3) She likes you but you don't like her, and 4) Neither of you fancy the other. Even if all seems to be going well, she will then just cut you off and disappear. It's impossible to meet people in a normal setting. Women don't go to pubs any more, they just sit at home swiping right or left, marking you as a 'possible' or a 'not worth bothering about'. It's very disheartening.'

I thought that sounded like a terrible way to hook up with someone you might want to spend the rest of your life with, aware of my own 'junk in the trunk', and thought back to my own dating days in the far-off 1950s.

We met boys at dances or in the newly opened coffee bars, drinking something called a 'cappuccino coffee' – how daring! Our parents were quite strict and every household would echo with the words handed down through the generations, 'Surely you're not going out dressed like that!' Forbidden makeup was hastily applied at the friend's house before we sneaked out to meet our 'crowd' at the coffee bar with the jukebox in the corner churning out current hits by Cliff Richard and Elvis Presley.

We were actually quite chaste in our behaviour and any canoodling was done usually in the back of a car with one couple in the front and another in the back. It was called 'necking', and appearing at school the following day with a love-bite on your neck was a testament to your popularity and daring. Girls might permit a bit of fondling 'above the waist' with only the slutty ones allowing anything 'below the waist'. Very few girls went 'all the way', meaning full intercourse. We judged a boy on how well he kissed and scored him 1 – 10, either too sloppy or nice. There were no 'tongues' – bleaurrr!

I was quite rebellious in those days. At age 15, like all the other girls in my class at school, I had a mad crush on Bill Carruthers, the son of the school's cook (yes, we had freshly cooked lunches every day). He was much older than me, at least 19, and had a *motorbike*. I was thrilled when he asked me to go to the cinema with him and I had my first ride on the back of his bike. Needless to say, when my father found out there were ructions and I was forbidden to see him again.

When Bill asked me out again, I told my parents I was going to my friend Sandra's house and my dad dropped me there in his car, saying he would come back and pick me up at 10. Sandra agreed to cover for me as I sneaked out to meet Bill. We just went for a coffee but got chatting with his friends and didn't realise the time. On the hurried journey back to Sandra's house on his motorbike, we stopped at some traffic lights and a car pulled up alongside. It was my dad, on his way to collect me. I was not allowed out for three weeks.

I was only 15 when I first met the man who was to become my husband. Our two families were staying at the same holiday hotel in Margate, Kent, and my mother pointed out Maurice and his brother Michael saying, 'They look like two nice boys' thus ensuring I disliked them on sight for that very reason. In those days, families all ate every meal together in the dining room of the hotel, having a cooked lunch and changing into smarter clothes in the evening for dinner. The teenagers would 'hang out' – although obviously we didn't use that term – in the basement, where there was a table tennis table and a jukebox, and we'd chat and jive.

In spite of my mother's judgment, I did like Maurice, although he was six years older than me which is a lot when you're 15. I mentioned there was a film I wanted to see called *The Girl Can't Help It*, starring rock 'n' roller Little Richard and Jayne Mansfield, and he said he would take me. I'd never been out with an older man before and asked my mother if I should offer to pay half of the ticket. She told me to buy him an ice-cream in the interval instead.

I got into his car and sat on a golf ball left on the front seat – he was obviously a keen golfer. Feeling a bit embarrassed, I slipped it into my bag as he walked round to the driver's side. I don't know if he enjoyed the film but I did, and he asked to see me again when we were home in London. We dated on and off for a while and he actually asked me to marry him when I was sixteen. Of course I said no; I mean, how could I marry a man who couldn't jive? It was unthinkable. I was that mature.

Two years later I came to my senses and we got engaged when I was eighteen. I still have that golf ball as a memento of our first date, and yes, bless him, he did learn to jive!

I decided to ask my friends how they met their husbands the next time we met on a Wednesday morning. It was at my home again and I made my special Apple-Amaretti tart which is a favourite with my family. I'll give you the recipe later.

'What, no lemon drizzle cake?' said Barbara and received one of my special looks that I reserve for people talking on their phones whilst at the checkout in the supermarket.

We all married young in those days, the average age for men being 22 and girls 20.

'I was 18 when I met Ronnie,' said Jess. 'He was what we called IDB – 'in Daddy's business'.

That was normal, for in the 50s it was assumed that a boy would follow in the same occupation as his father, either in retail, industry, down a coalmine or whatever. The girls were expected to marry a nice boy and produce grandchildren. Most parents, though, wanted their children to follow a profession, a doctor or a lawyer being the first choice. An accountant? Maybe. A hairdresser? Meh!

That reminded me of the Jewish joke where a proud grandmother was showing her friend a picture of her 'future doctor grandson' aged about a year. 'Can he walk?' asked the friend. 'Thank God he doesn't have to,' came the answer.

The others volunteered their stories:

'I met Brian when we were both acting in a play with our amateur dramatic society,' said Pauline, who carried her acting ambitions into quite a successful career. 'We were playing an Elizabethan drama and I was Queen Elizabeth I in a huge crinoline skirt which was quite heavy to wear. Brian was Sir Walter Raleigh, and we actually disliked each other, with each of us trying to upstage the other by overacting wildly during rehearsals. However, the night of the actual performance, we had a banqueting scene and, at the end of the meal, I stood up when a liveried footman pulled my chair back. Unfortunately, the bottom of my skirt got caught under the leg of the chair and, as he pulled it back, my skirt fell down and I was standing there in my knickers. Brian immediately swept his cloak in front of me, saying something like, 'Prithee ma'am, I'm here to serve thee', just giving me time to hoick it up, hoping the audience hadn't noticed too much. I had to marry him after that!'

'I was sitting outside a nightclub having a fag,' said Sheila DTR, 'when this guy came out and said, "Why are you sitting out here by yourself?" I told him because the band were rubbish, none of them could play, the boys were all drunk and my best friend had got off with some turnip-head from Luton. I asked what he did and he said he was the bass player with the band. Oops! We got married the following year.'

Barbara met her husband, Leonard, in the operating theatre of a children's hospital where he was a paediatric surgeon and she a nurse. 'He was taking out some kid's appendix,' said Barbara, 'and I was assisting. He said to me "pass me another swab" and our eyes met over our masks with this anaesthetised child being our only unconscious witness. We had a little snog in the sluice room, and that was that.'

We all agreed that was the most romantic thing we'd ever heard.

'I met Malcolm at Weight Watchers,' said Deely. We looked at her in disbelief.

'What happened?'

'He got thin and I got pregnant,' she said. 'You were supposed to eat for two in those days. There weren't any scans back then so I ate for four in case I was expecting triplets. Even the midwife was disappointed and said, "I thought there was more than one in there."'

We all looked at her. 'All right, I'll start on Monday,' she said. 'Now pass that apple thing.'

More coffee anyone?

16

It's only a car!

My friend Gloria loves her car. She loves, loves, *loves* her car! I don't know what breed it is but the current one is a low grey thing with a fat bottom. I say 'current' because she buys a new one every year and duly transfers her personal number plate on to the latest treasure. She pampers her car like a child, having it shampooed and hoovered and polished every week.

I'm terrified every time she gives me a lift because she barks out instructions at me before I even approach it: 'Check there's no mud on your shoes', 'Don't slam the door, shut it gently', 'Take your bag off the seat!', 'Don't get fingermarks on the dashboard.' Forget it – I'll walk! In the summer she takes the lid off so by the time we arrive at our destination my painstakingly straightened hair has turned into a halo of matted frizz.

For me, if a car has a wheel on each corner and a CD player and makes a noise when I turn on the ignition, meaning it works, then I'm happy. Not only do I not know the make of my car – I think it's a WV Something – the only way I can remember the number plate is by turning it into an acronym: DBC = Don't Buy Chocolate, followed by some number or other.

I know enough that when the red light on the dashboard goes on, I should put petrol in it. I'm quite good at that now, but the first time I did it I thought there was something wrong with the nozzle because it kept stopping and I kept pressing it until the petrol jumped out of the car over my shoes. I rely on the very efficient Government motoring department to remind me when my road tax is due, only they don't provide you with that little round paper disc to stick on your windscreen any more so I don't know how they know I've paid it.

If a tyre goes flat, a nice man from the RAC comes and puts another one on for me. I used to have a spare one in the boot (tyre that is, not nice RAC man, sadly) but they don't provide those anymore which is a bit mean. The last time he came to change the tyre, I said to him, 'What happens if I break down on my way to Tesco?' and he said, 'I'll come and get you, darling.' (I might have imagined that last bit, but he was *so* good-looking!)

I don't particularly like driving but consider myself to be reasonably proficient at it, although parking is not my strong point. After ten minutes of manoeuvring into a parking space one of the kids will inevitably say, 'That's fine Mum, leave it here, we'll walk to the kerb.' At least I don't do 'touch parking' like Deely: When backing into a parking space she reverses until she 'touches' the car behind, then edges forward until she 'touches' the car in front and repeats this until she is centred to her satisfaction.

The problem is the roads are so complicated nowadays. I've lived in this district all my life and there is a very busy junction that I have to use regularly. It's called

Henley's Corner and it used to be a straightforward cross-road controlled by traffic lights. If you wanted to go straight ahead, you did; if you wanted to turn right or left, you did. Simple as that. Then they took about a year to mess around with it and it is now the most convoluted arrangement of multiple lanes, slip roads and signposts, and impossible to negotiate. If you want to turn right and get in the wrong lane, you can find yourself on a motorway and end up in Birmingham.

Ah, motorways. I remember the first one opening to great fanfare in 1959, the M-bloody-1. I also remember the initial glimpse of this forbidding structure when I was with my husband and saw the huge sign stating: NO STOPPING. NO RIGHT TURN. DO NOT EXCEED 70mph. HARD SHOULDER FOR EMERGENCIES ONLY, and was scared just looking at it.

So you can imagine my heart-stopping fear when I found myself in the wrong lane of traffic, one day, and not able to manoeuvre into the slip road that ran alongside the lead-in to the motorway that I planned to take. Other than cause an accident, I had no option than to follow the lane of cars on to the motorway itself. I was terrified, not knowing where I was going or how I could get back. I started shaking, gripping the steering wheel so tight my hands went numb. A glance in the rearview mirror showed my face deathly white with cold sweat breaking out on my forehead. What a time to have my first panic attack when I was taking my youngest daughter, then aged five, to a birthday party with her little voice from the backseat bleating 'Are we nearly there?' every few minutes.

Eventually, of course, I came to a service station and was able to drive round and back the way I came. I managed to get us to the party, albeit a bit late, where Mr Whoopsie the Clown was in full swing, only to find that all the other mothers had adopted the latest fashion of long skirts flowing over knee-length boots, this being 1973, whilst I was still in my mid-thigh mini-skirt and feeling a total prat. It was not a good day!

If you've never had a panic attack, you cannot image how bad it actually is, and the feeling of trepidation never really leaves you. I'm OK driving most of the time, although I would never go on a motorway, and I drive around the most circuitous routes to avoid Henley's Corner, described earlier, taking twice as long to get anywhere – but at least I get there. To this day, if I'm going somewhere, say to a shopping mall, I have to go the same route every time. Any 'diversion' sign starts my stomach tightening again.

So I really needed that nice man from the RAC to come to my rescue on my way to my usual Tesco store. I was tootling happily along the main road, sticking firmly to the left-hand lane and singing along to Chuck Berry's *Riding Along in my Automobile* (ironically) which was blasting from the CD player. We had just got to the chorus – 'Hail, hail, rock and roll' – as I approached the slip road leading to the store, only to be confronted with a barrier with the ominous sign 'Road Closed'. NO! Oh God!

Kill the music! I was still on the main road, hemmed in by cars and lorries on either side with more thundering down another slip road from the flyover, and the sign for the dreaded M1 ahead! I could feel the familiar tightening of my throat and stomach and managed to edge over to the left, stopping the car in a sort of layby where I sat trembling, wondering what to do.

I noticed a huge truck which had pulled up behind me. I got out of my car and shakily approached the driver. His cab was at least twelve feet high and he opened the door and looked down enquiringly at me. I stammered, 'I need to go there,' pointing back, 'but the road is closed.'

'Is OK,' he said in a Polish accent. 'You drive on, stay in left-hand lane to the roundabout, then turn—' I wailed, 'I caaan't!' and burst into tears. Do you know what this lovely man did? He said, 'I show you,' and climbed down from his high perch, locked his door and got respectfully into the back of my car. This knight-in-shining-denim directed me along the main road, quite a long way, with me gripping the wheel and making whimpering noises – 'Uh, Uh, Uh,' – until we reached a point where we could double back, approaching the slip road from the other end.

Eventually, to my relief, I saw the Tesco sign and his huge truck ahead. I stopped the car and said, 'I'll be fine now,' and thanked him profusely, scrabbling in my bag to find a £5 note which he tried to refuse but I insisted he take. Fortunately, the railings were broken in several places so he could get back to his truck easily. There are some good people in the world. I was still shaking as I pushed the trolley round the aisles.

This didn't stop me driving, however, and that Wednesday I was due to go to Gloria's turned out to be one of those rare hot and humid days. I made my way there with my left hand ready to prevent the lemon drizzle cake, perched on the passenger seat, from sliding off as I went over the speed bumps. Although Gloria had agreed to host the Wednesday meeting, it was her housekeeper's day off and she wasn't prepared to bake today in case, God forbid, she had to wash up the food processor and load the cups into the dishwasher herself (yes, I know). So I promised to bring a cake to our get-together for her.

'What, again?' said Deely, scornfully looking at my – all right, slightly singed on one edge – offering. 'We'll start to sweat lemon drizzle if we eat any more of it.'

I explained it was the only one I had in the freezer. Then I told them what had happened on my fateful shopping trip and they were incredulous. 'He could have raped you!' they cried. Yeah, right. An 80-year-old wild-eyed, gibbering lunatic. An irresistible prospect for any man.

Thinking about it afterwards, I know that most people take great pride in their cars, and TV programmes like *Top Gear* used to attract millions of viewers. It's me who is the odd one – I do get that.

I remember when Gloria rang my doorbell and said, 'I've come to show you my new car.'

I said, 'Why?' and she looked at me in disbelief. 'It's fitted with Bluetooth,' she said proudly (being one of the first to get this connection) and, naturally, I didn't know what she was talking about. I still don't.

17

Exercise isn't just about burning calories

I went to visit Jess who was laid up in bed with a bad back. I felt sorry for her because she is sometimes in pain and her hip replacement operation didn't help. I offered to bring her a lemon drizzle cake but she declined – rather hastily, I thought – saying that she didn't feel like eating anything at the moment.

I asked if she was doing the exercises her physio had given her and she shrugged. 'She told me to stretch my leg out and pump it up and down. What good does that do?'

'It strengthens your quadriceps,' I explained, 'the big muscles in the front of your thigh. You should also hold on to something and gently swing your leg forward and back.' I could see I was talking to the wall.

I am a fitness instructor. I didn't intend to be one any more than I intended to become a writer. But you're reading this and I'm fit.

It's ironic really that even in my 80s I am still teaching a Body Conditioning class and clock up eight sessions of exercise a week when I hated exercise at school. I was always 'forgetting' to wear the regulation navy knickers so I could get out of gym and netball – which in the 1940s we did wearing just our white blouses and pants. I also arranged for my period to last three weeks out of every month.

It wasn't until I was in my 20s and had recently given birth to someone – I forget whom – that my mother tactfully suggested I do something about the extra three stone I had gained (doesn't everyone?) during the pregnancy. I only realised afterwards that new-born babies don't come out of the womb weighing three stone. I must have put on weight during labour.

My mother, so slim, stylish and beautiful, with clear blue eyes and unlined skin right up to her death at 91 (so where the hell did I come from?!) persuaded me to accompany her to her Keep Fit class in the local church hall, and to make sure I kept my word, she would pick me up the following week.

We arrived at the church hall and my mother introduced me to her friends and other participants: 'This is my (galumphing elephant of a) daughter who's coming to join us' and they nodded politely. Looking at them, I realised I had neglected to apply red lipstick, blue eye shadow and red polish on my fingernails. Mum then introduced me to the teacher who was the thinnest woman I have ever seen. She looked about 100 with spider legs in black tights and a little black mini-skirt round her bony waist over a leotard. There was another similar-aged (they were probably about 40) woman perched at an upright piano.

Spider-woman clapped her hands for attention, piano-lady started playing a jaunty tune, and the class began:

'Everyone walk round the room,' she called in a jolly voice and I walked round the room. 'Swiiing your arms' – I swung my arms. 'Now walk on tiptoe' – I walked on tiptoe, swinging my arms.

'Did you all remember to bring a silk scarf?' Er – no. Luckily, Mummy had a spare one.

'Now, hold the scarf and wave your arms above your head and swaaaay to the side and the other side.' I walked, I tiptoed, I swayed.

We touched our toes (I couldn't quite see mine), lay on our towels (Mummy had anticipated my forgetting that one as well), and kicked our legs up and down like prone Tiller Girls. Then it was time to go home.

'I'll meet you here next week,' said Mummy, pointedly, and I said OK.

I was late, mainly because I got lost and, although I had remembered to put on red lipstick, I had to go back and fetch my silk scarf. By the time I arrived, they had already walked, tiptoed and swayed. Spider-woman gave me a look, but allowed me to join in.

I didn't go the following week because – I just didn't. Then a miracle happened. At a party I got talking to a girl who was a professional dancer. She promised to take me to her jazz class, held in a studio just off Leicester Square, given by a choreographer called Robin Winbow. She warned me to stay at the back because it was a class for professional dancers, one of which I was obviously not!

I watched these lithe girls and boys limbering up at the barre and hid behind a pillar at the back. Robin was a neat, slim guy with a big smile and blond, floppy hair – this was the 60s remember. He started the class and, to my surprise, I wasn't too bad and could follow a few of the moves. That was it – I was hooked. I flung the children into school each morning and jumped on the tube to Leicester Square. Leaving the class afterwards, buzzing and exhilarated, I found I could cope cheerfully with whatever the rest of the day threw at me.

After a few months, my technique much improved and the excess weight gone as well as another further stone, I was proficient enough to move to the Dance Centre in Floral Street, Covent Garden. This was a magical place for an amateur like me. You could pass by a studio and catch a glimpse of the girls from the dance group Hot Gossip being put through their paces and peek into another studio where Pan's People were working out their dance routine for that evening's live performance on *Top of the Pops*. They were only told which song they would be dancing to on the day of transmission. No stress there!

I attended wonderful jazz classes run by choreographers like Arlene Phillips and Bruno Tonioli and made a lot of friends. We were heartbroken when the Dance Centre closed down but, soon afterwards, Pineapple Studios opened nearby and everyone flocked there.

Before that happened, however, something occurred that would change the course of my life. I was standing in a group of twenty people waiting for a class to begin when we were informed that the teacher hadn't turned up (it was neither of the above-mentioned). We all stood there wondering what to do, then I heard myself saying, 'I'll take the class,' and was handed the drum and padded stick which this particular teacher used instead of music. I remembered the routine from the day before and, to my surprise, they just followed me and it was fine. I actually got a round of applause at the end.

That decided me: I was going to become an exercise teacher and base my class on the style I'd learned and loved. I reckoned that ordinary women with no aspirations to be dancers still had a sense of rhythm, and I could teach a modified version of jazz dance, playing the same funky music but instead of using the dancers' language, 'Pliés in first position', I would say, 'Stand with your heels together, feet turned out and bend your knees.'

It worked. I enrolled in several teacher-training courses to learn about the various muscle groups and safe use of movement and, in 1982, opened my own Fitness Centre which I called All That Jazz, encompassing classes from aerobics to yoga. It was the first studio of its kind to open outside central London, apart from the church hall venues frequented by my mother, and long before exercise became mainstream and the current proliferation of gyms. I persuaded my favourite teachers from Pineapple to make the reverse tube journey that I normally took, from Leicester Square to my studio in North London, and they brought their own followers with them.

As word spread of the great classes on offer, I had to drag in my sister to sit at the door and take the money as I couldn't manage everything on my own. She agreed if I promised to play her favourite song in my class, which was *Get Down On It* by Kool & the Gang. I guess that song held some special memory for her, I don't know, but I really appreciated her help to deal with the influx of people pouring through the door. I often found myself teaching up to 90 in one class. It was a fun time and lasted for seven years, from 1982 until the day the whole building caught fire and burned down in 1989. But that's another story.

I wish I could stress how important exercise is, especially as you get older. Most of my friends in the Wednesday 'coffee 'n' cake' group do some sort of exercise, even, in Barbara's case, 'a bit of gardening'. Yoga and Pilates are the favourites, with a bit of energetic Body Conditioning or Zumba thrown in occasionally.

A recent report suggested that trying to lose weight by exercising alone doesn't work. Of course, it doesn't if you leave the gym then tuck into a bucket of fried junk food! But to suggest exercise is not a contributory factor in weight loss is also wrong. It is much more than that.

I get furious when people, even some medical people, suggest that you'd have to swim the length of the Thames to burn off the calories in a tomato. Comparisons like that are misleading, senseless, and would just put people off from bothering. The old equation of 'energy in, energy expanded' still holds strong when initially losing weight.

Exercise is so much more than burning calories. It is essential for your health, both mental and physical, and the benefits of doing it regularly will make all the difference to how you live your life as an older person. It takes a certain level of fitness to be able to do normal things. For example, you need:

Agility: Being able to climb up on a chair, then up on to the kitchen worktop to get the biscuit tin down from the high shelf where you have put it to stop yourself eating the contents. (How's that working for you?)

Strength: To be able to lift a three-year-old grandchild or heavy bags of shopping out of the car – though not at the same time!

Balance: So you don't fall flat on your face stepping into your knickers.

Suppleness: To be able to pick something up off the floor without doing your back in.

Flexibility: So you can twist round in the driving seat to check on the oncoming traffic before pulling out into a junction.

Those sorts of normal things.

Besides, exercise will also strengthen your heart and lungs, tone your muscles and improve your posture, as well as increasing the blood flow to your brain, thereby hopefully staving off dementia. What's not to like?

There is also another aspect that is often overlooked: the social side. The first time you pluck up courage to go to a Body Conditioning class, you probably will be a bit flummoxed by the steps, but it's like any sport, once you are familiar with the 'language' it becomes easy. The second time you go, you will recognise that side-cross-side step – oh yes, that's a grapevine – got that! The third time, the lady who smiled at you last week will say, 'Do you want to go for coffee after the class?' and suddenly you have a new friend.

Just do it, yeah? Take my mum's advice and get to a class. You don't have to wear red lipstick, honest! Just some leggings and a T-shirt. And it will keep you slim whatever the 'experts' say.

Get Down on It!

18

I'm not superstitious (touch wood!)

I have a confession to make: I'm a drug addict. I cannot exist without this substance and keep a supply in the living room where I watch TV, on the kitchen shelf so I have easy access, in my bedside drawer in case I wake in the night, another lot in my car and an emergency supply in my handbag. I don't know which addictive drug is used in lip balm, is it the phenol, salicylic acid or celyl alcohol? But the moment my lips feel dry or tingly, I reach for that little tube of instant relief.

I know it's probably just a habit that has turned into a superstition because I get edgy if I don't have a stash with me as I just know I will be conscious of my lips getting drier by the minute, even if they're not. I don't wear lipstick as I can't bear seeing the imprint of other people's on cups and discarded tissues.

I guess we all have these little idiosyncrasies and we discussed this at our usual Wednesday get-together at Laila's house. She'd made a lovely marble cake with real melted chocolate ensuring a suitably gungy texture. We all agreed that Laila was an exceptionally good baker and Jess suggested putting her forward as a contestant on the TV *Bake*

Off show – before one look at Laila's face and the threat of a hot cross bum!

We decided that superstition must be fear of something bad happening if we didn't follow some course of action to prevent it, and these rituals must have originated at a time when people believed in evil spirits and bad omens.

Pauline said hers was the necessity of knowing the exact location of the nearest loo wherever she went and has to look up her route on the internet before she leaves the house, or she's convinced she'll be 'in trouble'. Pauline confides in everyone she meets that she has a slight incontinence problem, in that when she feels the urge to wee, her body confirms this by releasing a small drop of urine to let her know. This is sometimes too much information for the newly introduced but that doesn't seem to bother her. I just hope she never receives an honour from the Queen or Prince Charles.

'I can give you directions from my house to anywhere in London,' she said, 'just by signposting the shops that will allow you to use their loo. In some places you have to buy a coffee so that the daily code is printed on the receipt, but some of the bigger stores are a nuisance because their loos are on the fifth or sixth floor and that means either you have to wait for the lift or trundle up the slow-moving escalator by which time, well – I'd need the lingerie department!'

'I wouldn't go in the lift,' said Sheila DTR, 'It's not so much claustrophobia as I don't like being in a room with a closed door. For some reason I'm OK in a plane but I avoid the tube because I think I'll be trapped when the doors close. I don't even shut my shower door when I'm in there. And it's getting worse. I know it's been ages since the restrictions of Covid were lifted, but after getting used to being in my house all that time I really have no desire to go anywhere, either to a noisy restaurant or a crowded theatre, which I used to love'. We all feel the same.

I recalled that my mother had a certain habit that if she left the house then had to go back inside for something she'd forgotten, she had to sit down and count to ten before leaving again. If she didn't do this, she might have an accident or worse. Superstitious nonsense, of course, but my sister and I still do this!

My own personal superstition means that I have to stand at my front door when my children or grandchildren leave and wave until they're out of sight. I'm sure this irritates them intensely, especially if they want to reset their satnav or send a text before driving off, when they realise I'm still standing there waving like an idiot who's spotted a TV camera. But that's too bad. My oldest granddaughter showed me a cartoon of an old lady waving, with the caption: 'If your grandmother doesn't wave to you when you leave her house, she's not really your grandmother.' I guess it's my superstitious way of holding them close and keeping them safe. If only …

Of course, the obvious superstitions are touching wood or throwing a pinch of salt over your shoulder to ward off bad luck. I read somewhere that in ancient times it was thought that trees harboured good and bad spirits which could be called upon or chased away by touching or knocking on something wooden.

Jess and Barbara disagreed about whether finding a penny brought good luck. Barbara said it did, but Jess said only if the penny is heads up. If it's tails up you should turn it over and leave it for the next person to find or you'll have bad luck. I didn't know that one.

Gloria said there must be different superstitions in other countries. 'I had an au pair once from Brazil who, whenever she swept the kitchen floor, made sure the children weren't in the room. When I asked why, she said that South Americans believe that if a broom sweeps over your feet you will remain single for the rest of your life. The curse can be broken if you spit on the broom. She wasn't sure how this originated, but legend has it that if a woman can't keep her house clean she won't make a good wife. Why is it always the women?'

At that moment, Laila's black cat Houdini (he keeps escaping) stalked majestically across the floor and we all agreed that would bring us good luck for the rest of the day. As it was nearly Christmas we decided to book a restaurant for all of us to celebrate the fact that we had made it through another year, in spite of Covid spewing out different variants at will. There were nine of us women plus the four of us who still had partners, which makes oh-oh, thirteen – we can't have that!

This one apparently had its origin in Judas Iscariot's being the thirteenth member of the particular dinner party that led to Christ's crucifixion. I believe it was a Passover meal so eating all that Matzoh must have upset Judas's tummy and put him in a bad mood. I get that. In our family, if my parents invited friends for dinner and the number added up to thirteen, they would insist our Irish nanny join the table, much to her discomfort.

Gloria solved the problem. 'Don't worry,' she said, 'I'm off to Miami next week, fingers crossed, so you'll be OK. In the meantime, I'd like you all to come outside to see my new car.'

More cake anyone?

19

90 is old enough for me

Some years ago, I popped in to visit my 92-year-old Auntie Sonia in her excellent care home, taking her favourite chocolate buttons. The receptionist told me she was in the exercise class. I peeped through the door and spied her sitting in her wheelchair in a circle with all the other wheelchair-bound residents. I waved to her, but she didn't respond as she was suffering from advanced Alzheimer's and had long forgotten who I was. In fact, she didn't know where she was or what day it was and couldn't read, follow a television programme or even feed herself.

I watched the two resident physios standing in the middle of the circle encouraging their charges to catch a soft ball and throw it back to them, and while some attempted to comply, most, who had obviously suffered a stroke or were mentally impaired like Auntie Sonia, just slumped in their wheelchairs waiting for the next event of the day, probably lunch.

It struck me forcibly that I did not want to end up like these unfortunate people. Is this inevitable? Most probably yes, as my mother, Auntie Sonia's sister, and *their* mother, my grandmother, all had dementia, which does not bode well for me! I decided then and there that 90 was going to be my cut-off point and once I reach that age – if I do – I would like to go and be with my husband, who died seven years ago and whom I miss terribly.

Don't get me wrong, I am not suicidal. In spite of my 80-plus years, I am lucky enough to be strong and healthy and enjoying the positive reaction to my last book *Getting Old, Deal with It*. Ironically, I was even featured in an episode of the ITV programme *Tonight*, entitled *How to Age Well*. So why would I want to do away with myself at 90? The main reason lay in front of my eyes: if I follow my maternal line of cognitive decline, in a few years' time it could be me in that wheelchair having to be hoisted from bed to the loo then to the shower where a dedicated carer would wipe and wash me before wheeling me to the dining room to shovel some mush into my mouth for breakfast. No thanks. I would rather go at a time of my own choosing while I still have all my faculties and can fend for myself.

There is a glimmer of hope on the horizon – or rather the glimmer of a glimmer of hope. In July, 2021, the US Food and Drug Administration finally gave approval to a drug called Aducanumab, also known as Aduhelm, which has been proved to slow down the progression of Alzheimer's disease. For the first time there is a drug that can break down the toxic protein called amyloid which clogs up the brain of Alzheimer's sufferers and is thought to cause tangles of a substance called tau. There is still a long way to go before this will be able to benefit the general population, and although it's been approved in the US that doesn't mean to say that it will be endorsed by the Medicines and Healthcare Products Regulatory Agency (MHRA) in this country. But we can only hope, or as my friends would say, 'fingers crossed'.

Another glimmer of hope is that politicians are now willing to listen to the pleas of terminally ill people for a change in the law to allow assisted dying, which, at the time of writing, incurs a penalty of fourteen years imprisonment.

A Private Member's Bill for England and Wales has been brought before Parliament, under the terms of which a patient with a terminal illness could apply to be helped to die at a time and place of their choice – for example, in their own home, with their family around them. Who wouldn't want that? Obviously there will have to be stringent safeguards, and many people will object, but at least it's being discussed now.

I do hope this Bill goes through. I truly believe that in 50 years this period of time will be looked back upon with incredulity, it being akin to a dentist refusing to numb a mouth during a tooth extraction or denying pain relief to a woman in labour. Unbelievable.

I sense more and more people are coming round to a change in the law, but where does that leave someone like me who isn't, fortunately, terminally ill? I promised my husband that I would stick around long enough to see our beloved grandchildren grown-up and living their own lives and that will have been accomplished by the time I'm 90.

I believe there comes a time when everyone reaches a point when they think, 'OK, I've had a good, long life with many blessings and the inevitable sorrows, but it's now time to leave the party'. There's a sense of creeping physical frailty, of increasing cognitive decline, and medical ailments which can only multiply as the years go by. How much these curtail one's standard of living is purely personal. Some people are content to continue with a life of permanent disability and still find joy in their lives well into old age and that is entirely their choice. It just wouldn't be for me as I believe in quality of life rather than longevity. Why people think it's such a big deal to look forward to a birthday card from the Queen at age 100, I have no idea. I wonder if she'll send one to herself should she emulate her mother and live to a ripe old age?

I was 45 years old when my dad died in 1984, aged 72. As I stood beside my mother and sister at his graveside, my eyes kept reverting to the rectangular patch of grass alongside the dug grave, reserved for my mother when we purchased the double plot. I remember thinking to myself how must my mum feel looking at that and knowing that one day she would be under that patch of grass next to him. At the time it felt really weird and didn't happen until nearly 20 years later.

Now in my 80s, I look at a similar patch of grass next to my husband's grave and think, 'that's fine, my body will be lying next to him as it was for 56 years, and I hope his soul will be waiting to reunite with me in heaven – or from wherever he is sending me white feathers and the occasional red butterfly to settle next to me for a chat'. (Don't scoff, you don't know what you don't know.)

So how can I achieve my aim? At the moment I haven't a clue. I've done all the obvious things like issue instructions via a Power of Attorney that should I succumb to dementia or a stroke, thereby rendering me incapable of speech,

I would not want to be resuscitated if I got an infection etc., but that's not enough. I said to my 20-something grandson, 'Darling, will you find a way to bump me off when I get to 90?' He wisely said, 'Why don't you wait till you get there and see how you feel?'

Maybe I'll employ the same solution as I do when I want to wake up at a certain time. You know, when you repeat '7.30' several times before you fall asleep and your subconscious mind wakes you at that time. If I say firmly, 'You're 90 now, off you pop,' will that work?

Unfortunately, I've never liked the taste of alcohol but I suppose I could take up smoking. Can I blag a fag off someone to try? How about a spliff? What *is* a spliff? I've never understood recreational drugs but I know you need a 'dealer'. Could I find one in the Yellow Pages? (Grandchild: 'what's that?') Anyone got any spare Tramadol? Diamorphine? Midazolam? Anyone? I'm JOKING!

I decided to ask my friends what they thought at one of our 'coffee 'n' cake' meetings on Wednesday morning. It was at my house again and, just for a change, I had made their favourite cheesecake to give me the courage to ask the difficult question. (Actually, I'm not good at cheesecake so I'd asked my sister to make it for me – hers is delicious. Don't say anything.)

So – ladies – how would you choose to die? The answers were as I expected:

'I wouldn't'

'Why are you asking that?'

'I don't want to think about it'

'Can we talk about something else?'

But it's going to happen one day – to all of us. Even TV personality Jeremy Clarkson said, 'Dying is like going to the dentist's or buying a Volvo. We all get around to it sooner or later.'

So, come on, what do you say? One of you, start them off:

'OK, I'd like to die in my sleep with my cat, Brenda, curled up beside me – without suffering any debilitating illness beforehand of course.'

'I'd like to collapse on the golf course like Bing Crosby – or was it Bob Hope? I can never remember.'

'I'd like to be in hospital hooked up to every drug going.'

'Drunk, sloshed, legless – just a couple of glasses more than usual, actually.'

'On a sunbed, by a pool in St Tropez.'

'Mid-orgasm, then I could come and go at the same time!' (Sorry, Reader.)

'Joan Rivers had it right. You go in for a facelift and don't wake up. So for me, it's under an anaesthetic.'

'Under no circumstances!'

'Under Brad Pitt.'

'Under a spreading chestnut tree.'

'Underneath the arches.'

'By the light of the silvery moon.'

'Old Man River.'

OK, forget I asked! Maybe I'll just have to wait until I'm 90 and see how I feel after all.

More coffee anyone?

20

Ready – set – BAKE

A few people who read this book in draft form before it was published asked me for the recipes for some of the cakes mentioned in these pages. I'm quite happy to do this so please have a go at anything you fancy. In fact, why don't you copy us and invite two or three friends and neighbours in for a regular get-together and chat?

Talking about recipes, like most bakers we tend to juggle around with the quantities of the ingredients to get the desired result we want. So, if some of the quantities seem strange to you, you can always adjust them yourself. I promise you they taste all right.

I also have to mention that oven temperatures vary. For example, my own gas oven was very spiteful when I first got it and every cake came out burnt on top and raw inside. I once made a fruit cake that must have been in the oven too long and came out like a solid block; my son said he would take it home to use as a doorstop.

I've always used gas and all these recipes are baked in a pre-heated oven at gas mark 4 which you can convert if your oven is electric. Likewise, all the measurements in these recipes will be in lbs and oz. I'm old, what do you want?!

I might not give you all the recipes: for example, Sheila's Honey Cake needs so many ingredients – I counted 17, which doesn't include sultanas which some people add – most of which are only available at stores like Waitrose, and is such a faff that, honestly, you'd be better off buying one.

Similarly, Deely's Clementine Cake is Nigella's recipe, so if you want that, you'll have to ask her.

I asked the other Sheila how she made those unusual *Hamantaschen* pastries and she admitted that, actually, her sister-in-law made them and she didn't like to ask her for the recipe, which is apparently a closely guarded secret.

Anyway, bake, share with family and friends and enjoy. What could be nicer?

The recipes

My Famous Lemon Drizzle Cake

This is for a standard 8-inch cake tin, greased or lined with greaseproof paper or some other non-stick parchment.

6oz soft butter or marge (I use Stork)
9oz self-raising (SR) flour
9oz caster sugar
3 eggs
Pinch of salt
6 tablespoons milk
Grated rind of a large lemon

For the drizzle:
5 tablespoons icing sugar, 5 tablespoons lemon juice

Beat butter and sugar together till creamy, add eggs one at a time with a spoonful of flour plus pinch of salt, in 3 goes, beating well each time to stop it curdling, then add milk, lemon rind and remaining flour.

Bake for 50 minutes and test by sticking a skewer in to see that it's cooked.

For the drizzle: warm the lemon juice and icing sugar in a pan till the sugar melts and it thickens slightly – don't allow it to boil. Prick the cake all over with a fork and pour the liquid over it so that it sinks into the holes.

Apple Amaretti Tart (Delish!)

This is for a 10–12 inch loose-bottomed flan case, the base lined with greaseproof paper, or similar non-stick stuff.

For the base:
8oz plain flour
Pinch of salt
4oz butter or marge
4oz caster sugar
3oz Amaretti biscuits crushed fairly small

For the topping:
4 or 5 even-sized Bramley apples
1oz caster sugar
2oz butter, melted
Half a teaspoon cinnamon

Pre-heat oven, gas mark 4 (or equivalent for your oven). Put flour and salt in a bowl, rub in butter, stir in sugar and crushed biscuits. Or do what I do and put the whole lot in a food processor and whizz it all together into a crumble.

Spread the mixture loosely and evenly on to the base of the flan, don't press it in. Peel and cut apples into quarters and remove core. Cut each quarter thinly into 8 or 9 slices (do this by hand) and spread in concentric circles around the base, covering all of it. Brush the melted butter over the apples. Mix the cinnamon with the caster sugar and sprinkle on top.

Bake for an hour till apples are soft and the edges tinged slightly brown.

This is fab and looks very impressive. I prefer to freeze it, thereby making it easier to peel off the greaseproof paper before defrosting. Enjoy.

Laila's Excellent Chocolate Roulade

After lighting the gas mark 4, line a baking sheet about 12ins × 8ins with greaseproof paper, making it large enough to overhang the edges.

2 eggs, separated
8oz caster sugar
7oz plain chocolate
Icing sugar
½ pint whipping cream
Few drops vanilla essence
8oz fresh or frozen raspberries, thawed

Beat the egg yolks, add the caster sugar gradually, beating until the mixture is pale and thick.

Melt 6oz of chocolate in 3 tablespoons of hot water, preferably in a bowl on top of a saucepan of boiling water. Stir gently and beat into the egg mixture. With clean beaters, whisk egg whites until they hold peaks, and fold into egg mixture.

Pour on to sheet, spread and bake for about 20 minutes, until top is just firm. Cool on sheet and chill in fridge.

Spread a sheet of clingfilm on the kitchen work surface and turn out roulade on top. Pull away the greaseproof paper gently.

Whip cream, flavour with vanilla essence and sweeten lightly with icing sugar; fold raspberries into the cream. Melt remaining chocolate and trickle over the roulade. Let it set, then spread the raspberries and cream evenly on top.

Roll up the roulade lengthways, using the clingfilm to help tip and mould it into shape, handling as little as possible. (Good luck with that!) Don't worry if it cracks a bit, that's normal. Carefully lift it on to serving dish and sprinkle with icing sugar.

Barbara's Easy-Peasy Yoghurt Cake

As Barbara says, this is the easiest cake ever as it only requires you to wash up one bowl afterwards – apart from the cake tin of course – and there is no weighing or measuring.

Take a small carton of plain or flavoured yoghurt (she uses Müller vanilla or toffee flavour, 160g), tip the contents into a bowl and wash out the carton. You are going to use this as a measure.

1 carton vegetable oil
2 cartons caster sugar
3 cartons SR flour
1 carton raisins and chopped-up glacé cherries
3 eggs

Do this first: Measure out the 'dry' ingredients like sugar into one bowl and the flour into another. This is to save you washing out the yoghurt carton after filling it with oil. Now you're ready to put the whole thing together.

Beat the eggs thoroughly, preferably with an electric whisk. Add the oil and beat again. (You can now chuck the greasy carton). Add the sugar and whisk till the mixture thickens a bit. Add the yoghurt and dried fruit. Lastly, stir in the flour.

Bake for 50 minutes to 1 hour, according to your oven.

Jess's Cheeky Cinnamon Buns

The ingredients for this one are actually in grams.

300g SR flour
2 tablespoons caster sugar
1 teaspoon cinnamon
Pinch of salt
70g butter, melted
2 egg yolks
130ml milk, plus a bit extra for glazing

For the filling
1 teaspoon ground cinnamon
55g light-brown soft sugar
2 tablespoons caster sugar
40g butter, melted

First: Line a baking sheet with greaseproof paper.

Mix the flour, caster sugar and cinnamon together with a pinch of salt in a bowl.

Whisk the butter, egg yolks and milk together and combine with the dry ingredients to make a soft dough. Turn out onto a floured surface and roll out to a rectangle, about 30 × 25cm.

Then make the filling, mixing all the ingredients for it together. Spread evenly over the dough, then roll it up lengthways, like a Swiss roll, to form a log.

Using a sharp knife, cut the dough into 8 even-sized slices and lay them on the baking sheet. Brush gently with the extra milk and bake for 30–35 minutes or until golden brown.

Pauline's Great Ginger Cake
with Lemon Icing

7oz SR flour

7oz caster sugar

1 teaspoon ground ginger (Pauline adds 2 teaspoons)

1 teaspoon bicarbonate of soda

2oz margarine

1 egg, beaten

2 tablespoons golden syrup

9 fluid oz hot water

For the icing:
3oz icing sugar, juice of a large lemon

Grease and line a baking tin, 11 × 7 inches.

Mix the flour, sugar, ginger and bicarb together in a bowl. Using your fingers, rub the margarine in until the mixture resembles breadcrumbs. Add the beaten egg, syrup and hot water and mix well with a wooden spoon till it looks smooth.

Pour mixture into the tin and bake for 35–40 minutes or until springy to the touch. Leave to cool in the tin.

When cold, sieve the icing sugar into a bowl and add the juice of the lemon, stirring till it's mixed. You may need to add a little water if necessary. Spread over the cake.

Laila's Marvellous Marble Cake

8oz butter or marge (Laila uses Stork)
8oz caster sugar
12oz SR flour with pinch of salt
4 eggs
4oz dark chocolate
1 extra ounce butter

Prepare an 8-inch cake tin lined with greaseproof paper.

Put marge and sugar into a food processor and whizz together till light and fluffy (or beat together in a bowl). Break the eggs into a separate bowl and whisk them, preferably with an electric whisk. Add the beaten egg with some of the flour (to stop it curdling) to the food processor in 4 goes, beating thoroughly each time. Once that is all mixed in, put **half** the mixture in the tin in dollops.

Melt the chocolate with the extra ounce of butter either in a bowl over a pan of boiling water or in the microwave. Add this melted chocolate to the remaining mixture in the food processor and whizz together. Put dollops of this on top of the plain mixture in the tin. Then with a knife, draw it through the mixture several times to create a marble effect.

Bake, gas mark 4 or equivalent, for 50 minutes. If, when you test it, a skewer comes out slightly sticky, that's fine.

My Sister's Old-fashioned Cheesecake

When I asked my sister for this recipe, she handed me a scrap of paper with scrawled writing on it with half the measurements missing and covered with blobs of cake mixture. She admitted she hasn't looked at the recipe for ages as she's been making this cake for about 40 years and can do it with her eyes shut. But, as she says, 'the old ones are the best'. True.

1lb curd cheese, which used to be known as cooking cheese
    (get this at a decent deli)
6oz caster sugar
3 eggs
10 digestive biscuits
2 × 150g pots of soured cream, whipped with 2oz caster sugar

Line an 8in cake tin with greaseproof paper. She uses a square tin.

Put the digestive biscuits into a polythene bag and bash them with a rolling pin until they form crumbs. Spread these evenly on the base of the tin.

Beat the eggs. Put the cheese, caster sugar and beaten egg in a bowl and beat together well till light and fluffy. Pour mixture over the biscuit crumbs and smooth the surface.

Bake for 30 minutes, or a little longer if the centre looks a bit wobbly, but don't overcook. Let it stand for 15 minutes while you whip the soured cream with the sugar. Spoon this on top of the cake and return to the oven for a further 10 minutes.

Turn off the oven and leave the cake in there until it cools. (Don't forget about it!)

My sister decorates it with strawberries cut in half. Looks good, tastes fab.

Ready – set – EAT!

Acknowledgements

The Daughter. I want to thank my brilliant oldest daughter, Sharon Pink for her continuing love, patience and support for everything I do, from checking my text ('You can't put that!') to answering my panic phone-calls when my computer plays up. Sharon, you are a very special girl and I love you more than words can say.

The Manuscript Doctor. What would I do without Wanda Whiteley who guides me towards the right path with every book I write, advising me what works and what doesn't – and she's always right. Her advice has been invaluable and this book wouldn't have been produced without her. Thank you, Wanda – I'm truly grateful to you.

The illustrator. Jacqui Caulton designed the lovely cover and formatted the pages of my script into an actual book. Thank you Jacqui, you're a true artist and I love what you've done.

The Reader. Thank you, dear Reader, for buying this book. I have mentioned in these pages that Alzheimer's disease is prevalent in my family and I have pledged to donate 50% of all proceeds from this book to Alzheimer's Research UK. So, Reader, here's the deal: if this book made you smile

– and I hope it did – please will you tell your friends about it so that we can all contribute to finding a cure for this horrible disease. Thank you so much.

Available from: **www.Amazon.co.uk/books**.

Also by Lee Janogly:

Getting Old, Deal with It

Mensch Publishing

ISBN: 978-1912914036

1

Are you old?

Have you ever stood behind an old, old person at the checkout in a supermarket? She watches as the cashier helpfully packs her shopping for her, whilst chatting happily about the weather and how it affects her arthritis.

Once her purchases are safely in her tartan wheelie bag she stands there expectantly until it dawns on her: Oh yes, she has to pay for it! There's a surprise. Only then does she dive into her cavernous bag to find her purse – her Clubcard – rummage, rummage, now where is it? It should be – maybe it's in the zippered compartment – Oh, what have we here, some money-off coupons! Are these still valid? No dear, they expired three months ago – and anyway, these are for Boots and this is Tesco. Really? Oh, what a shame. She peers at the display then counts out her coins to the exact penny, while you jiggle and fume with irritation. Don't. One day will probably be you.

Or me. I have to confess I'm the one holding up the queue at the cinema in front of the machine, trying to extract my pre-ordered tickets which it is reluctant to part with – or give me back my credit card. Or did I insert my travel card by mistake? Maybe. That is also me calling loudly for a human assistant at the self-service checkout in the supermarket to try and quell the infernal bleating of the voice insisting 'there is an unidentified object in the bagging area'. CAN I GET SOME HELP HERE? What? Oh, it's my umbrella. Sorry.

Me, old? Nah.

You may have noticed another sign: that whenever you are talking to an older person, whatever the subject, she will eventually contrive to inject her age into the conversation, whether it's relevant or not. 'Yes, airports are a nightmare today, you have to walk for miles to get to the gate, but I can manage even though (pause for maximum effect) I'm 73 you know'. The pride with which they say this leaves you no choice but to stagger back in amazement and tell them it's not possible as they look no older than 40. You lie.

It seems that everyone wants to BE the oldest and LOOK the youngest. They get so used to the faux surprised and complimentary comments about how young they look that eventually when asked their age, they craftily add a year, such as 'Next year I'll be 74' No! Really?!

The obvious lesson to be learned here is never ask anyone to guess your age. They may get it right! 'I don't look 73, do I?' (Not anymore!)

I think we're all deluded about our age depending on our mood or whether we had a good night's sleep. I know that sometimes I can look in the mirror and think 'You know what, you don't look bad'. Other times, particularly after a late night which included some sugary dessert followed by a bar of Cadbury's finest, the same mirror shows a raddled, puffy old hag with lines and wrinkles that definitely weren't there the day before. Some mirrors are just like that.

Printed in Great Britain
by Amazon

82207483R10092